Cardijn Studies: On the Church in the World of Today

Cardijn Studies: On the Church in the World of Today
Volume 1, Number 1, 2017

The *Cardijn Studies* journal is a refereed journal which aims to document the history of the Jocist, Cardijn inspired, lay movements both historically and in the present day as well as the examining the rich tradition of Catholic Social teaching on the church in the world of today. Articles cover a range of areas: the spirituality, methodology and the history of these traditions and movements in the church and in society.

Business Manager

Mr Hilary Regan, Publisher, ATF Press Publishing Group, PO Box 504, Hindmarsh, SA 5007, Australia. Email: hdregan@atf.org.au

Subscription Rates (2017)

Print	On-line	Print and On-line
Local – Individual Aus$35,	Local – Individual Aus$30,	Local – Individual Aus$55,
Institutional Aus$45	Institutional Aus$40	Institutional Aus$65
Overseas – Individuals US$30,	Overseas – Individual US$25,	Overseas – Individual US$50,
Institutional US$45	Institutional US$35	Institutional US$50

Cardijn Studies: On the Church in the World of Today is published by ATF Press Publishing Group, which is owned by ATF (Australia) Ltd (ABN 90 116 359 963) and is published at least once a year.
ISSN 2203-4587

Published by:

An imprint of the ATF Press Publishing Group owned by ATF (Australia) Ltd.
PO Box 504
Hindmarsh, SA 5007
ABN 90 116 359 963
www.atfpress.com
Making a lasting impact

Cardijn Studies:
On the Church in the
World of Today

Adelaide

Table of Contents

Editorial

Welcome to the first edition of Cardijn Studies, named for the late Belgian priest and cardinal, Joseph Cardijn, founder of the *Jeunesse Ouvrière Chrétienne* or JOC movement known in English as the Young Christian Workers or YCW.

As the title suggests, the aim of the journal is to provide a platform for publishing research relating to Cardijn, the JOC and other specialised Catholic Action movement.

The subtitle 'On the Church in the world of today' is evidently a reference to the title of *Gaudium et spes*, the Vatican II Pastoral Constitution on the Church in the World of Today, which canonised the Cardijn see-judge-act method.

Why an academic journal? First, research has long been lacking both on Cardijn himself, as well as the JOC and its sister movements, particularly outside the francophone world. This is reflected, for example, in the virtual absence of any significant reference to Cardijn's role at Vatican II in the reference five volume *History of Vatican II* edited by Giuseppe Alberigo and Joseph Komanchak (for the English edition).

Second, a slight revival of academic interest in these issues may have already begun, as indicated by several recent doctoral theses. The election of Pope Francis and his open adherence to the Cardijn see-judge-act method may be one of the factors here.

Indeed, it is clear that much of Francis' theology and praxis was directly influenced and inspired by Argentine priests and bishops formed by the specialised Catholic Action movements, including Lucio Gera, Rafael Tello, Juan Carlos Scannone SJ and the martyred Bishop Enrique Angelelli.

Yet much of the existing and new research remains hidden away in university libraries, and/or available only in the original language of the writer. Nor is there any network that aims to place such researchers in contact with each other.

In addition, much research in these areas does necessarily fall neatly in traditional academic categories. Indeed, lay apostolate and (specialised) Catholic Action in the sense understood and promoted by Cardijn lies precisely at the intersection of Church and world. It may therefore involve the theological, spiritual, philosophical, pedagogical, psychological or sociological fields or even a cross-cutting combination of these.

Cardijn Studies, therefore, aims to respond to these challenges to be the best of our ability by providing a platform for sharing research in these areas.

We are particularly pleased to be able to launch this journal to coincide with the 50th anniversary of Cardijn's death on 24 July 1967. Given his enormous contribution to Vatican II, it is a great paradox that he and the Specialised Catholic Action movements modelled on the JOC have lost their prominence in the decades since the Council.

Our publisher and editorial team

Thanks first of all to **Hilary Regan** from ATF Press for accepting the challenge to publish this journal. Hilary himself is a former Tertiary YCS leader from Adelaide with a long standing commitment to the Cardijn lay apostolate.

Other members of our editorial team are:

- **Assistant Professor Kevin Ahern**, Manhattan College, New York, Theological Ethicist and Director of Peace Studies, and International President of the International Catholic Movement for Intellectual and Cultural Affairs (ICMICA-Pax Romana);
- **Dr Ana Maria Bidegain**: Originally from Uruguay, where she was a member of the JUC while as student, she completed her PhD at Louvain-la-Neuve before beginning her academic career in Colombia. Currently she is professor of Latin American religions at Florida International University.
- **Fr Michael Deeb OP**, a South African-born former chaplain to the International Movement of Catholic Students (IMCS) and

International YCS, who now represents the Dominican community at the United Nations;

- **David Moloney**, professional historian, Cardijn Community Australia executive member,
- **Assistant Professor Bob Pennington** from Mt St Joseph University, Cincinnati, USA;

This issue

The main content for this issue is drawn from a Study Day on the theme 'History and memories of the Cardijn movements in Australia' organised by the Cardijn Community Australia on the campus of Yarra Theological Union in Melbourne on 26 October 2013.

The model chosen for that event was to invite presentations from both academics and from those who had practical experience of the Cardijn movements.

On the academic side, we present several papers dealing with the origins of the Cardijn movements in Australia.

Historian David Kehoe has a paper on the role of Kevin T Kelly, a public servant and diplomat, who worked for several years to launch the YCW to Australia after learning of its existence from a copy of the 1930 Manuel de la JOC that he received from France.

Catholic Theological College lecturer Fr Max Vodola follows with a paper on the contribution of Archbishop Justin Simonds, who may well have personally encountered Cardijn while studying at Louvain as the JOC rose to prominence during the late 1920s.

Yarra Institute for Religion and Society director, Fr Bruce Duncan CSsR, delivered a paper on Fr Frank Lombard, the Melbourne priest who became the driving force in the launch of the YCW and whose fiftieth death anniversary also falls this year.

Dr Peter Price, lecturer at the of Melbourne Yarra Theological Union, presented a paper on John Molony, a prominent YCW chaplain and theologian from Ballarat, who later became professor of history at the Australian National University.

In his paper, former Labor government minister, Dr Race Mathews, highlighted the connections between Cardijn and Fr Josemaria Arizmendiarrieta, the Basque priest who founded the Mondragon worker cooperatives in Spain.

My own paper sought to illustrate the theoretical foundations behind Cardijn's famous trinomial expressions of which the most famous is the see-judge-act.

On a more practical level, Professor Helen Praetz offered a series of suggestions for future researchers based on an earlier project of her own while Dr Melissa Walsh outlined the work of the Australian YCW Archives (the later not include in this volume).

Finally, and no less importantly, we present summaries of talks given from a participant point of view. Thus, Kevin Peoples, a former YCW leader from western Victoria, contrasts the methods of Cardijn and the Catholic Action leader, BA Santamaria.

John Finlayson shared his experiences as a YCW leader who started a team in a factory which led to a meeting with Cardijn during the latter's 1966 visit to Australia and who later became a prominent youth worker who helped launch Australia's first legal aid service.

The volume concludes with a book review of Race Mathews' *Of Labour and Liberty, Distributism in Victoria 1891–1966*.

Special thanks to David Molony for bringing these papers together in this issue for publication.

Future issues

Our next issue will draw primarily on another study day entitled 'Cardijn et le rayonnement jociste à Vatican II' focusing on the role of Cardijn and other jocist and specialised Catholic Action-formed periti, bishops and lay auditors at the Council.

In future, we look forward to organising or collaborating with further such events.

We also welcome papers and contributions from other researchers and authors.

Kevin Thomas Kelly, Prophet of the Australian YCW

David Michael Kehoe

The principal bearer of the doctrine of the Fr Joseph Cardijn's Jeunesse Ouvriere Chretienne (JOC) to Australia was Kevin Thomas Kelly, a young Melbourne public servant and an early and active member of the Melbourne-based lay intellectual group, the Campion Society. He was the prophet of the JOC and 'specialised' Catholic Action in Melbourne and Australia.

Kelly's evangelism had also led to Jocist ideas being adopted as the philosophy of Catholic Action in Australia. This happened when the Australian bishops adopted 'Specialised' Catholic Action in February 1939.[1] This enabled Jocism to become the official philosophy of Catholic Action movements in Australia. Without this, the Melbourne YCW and other Jocist movements would not have got off the ground.

Kelly's contribution lead eventually to a group of young priests establishing the first and most influential Jocist movement in Australia, the Melbourne YCW, with five parish groups by February, 1940 (official recognition was not until 10 October 1940). Fr Frank Lombard, who had been experimenting with the Jocist method in Northcote for about six months since mid-1939, was the founder and driving influence of what became this Melbourne YCW Priests Committee. Others key priests were Fr Vin Arthur in North Melbourne, Fr John F Kelly in West Melbourne and Fr Tom Murray.[2] Under the

---

1. Report of first National Conference of Diocesan Organisers of Catholic Action, Instaure Omnia in Christo, 20–27th February, 1939, 4, Catholic Action' Box, MDHC.
2. The Chaplain 1, 9, December 1940, p1 and 2, 7, November-December 1941, 7. See also, *Advocate*, 7/11/1940, 24, 20/2/1941, 21, and 2/10/41, 29. Also Ginnane, W, Ten Years of YCW in Australia, 1950, in MSS no 88, National YCW (Boys), YCW Headquarters Collection, Melbourne.

name of the Catholic Boys Legion, a youth organisation which the YCW priests committee had taken over from within, the Melbourne YCW was established as the official Catholic Action organisation for young working boys between the ages of fourteen and eighteen in the Archdiocese of Melbourne.

The name of this Jocist young worker movement was changed in late September, 1941 from 'Catholic Boys Legion' to 'Young Christian Workers'.

The Young Christian Students and the National Catholic Girls Movement (later the YCW for Girls) were established in Melbourne at the time of the Melbourne YCW or soon after, but by priests other than those of the Melbourne YCW Priests Committee. Their establishment and *modus operandi* came more directly from the bishops' Australian National Secretariat of Catholic Action whereas the Melbourne YCW, while authorised by this secretariat, was more the direct child of the Melbourne Priests Committee, and was thus in its early stages able to adopt a more complete version of Belgian Jocism than other early Jocist movements.

'Italian' and 'Specialised' Catholic Action

The term 'Catholic Action' was first used in connection with the religious, political and social movement which developed in the latter half of the nineteenth century in Italy. Italian Catholic Action aimed to defend the Pope and the Faith by supporting Catholic candidates in government elections and reviving Catholic liturgical and sacramental practice among negligent Catholics.[3] The means to achieve these objectives was organisation along the lines of age and sex. (The only exception being separate organisations for students.

The phrase 'Specialised Catholic Action' entered the debate on the nature of Catholic Action with the publication of Monsignor Pierre Bayart's L'Action Catholique Specialisee in 1935. Mgr Bayart's ideas drew completely from the writings of Fr Cardijn and Pius XI.[4] The organisation of the new Catholic Action was to be determined directly by its apostolic ends and not by a vaguely perceived politi-

---

3. NCE, volume 3, 262.
4. Bayart P, Specialised Catholic Action, transl. Fr J Smith, 55 (Melbourne, 1945) ANSCA, especially parts II and III, 5–15.

cal end, as in Italian Catholic Action. The danger in Italian Catholic Action was that the faithful would come to think that the main field of Church action was political, when its first field was the soul and its formation to prepare for the social and political battle.[5]

However, in the saga of Catholic Action's introduction into Australia in the 1930s and 40s, the Jocist basis of Specialised Catholic Action was not fully appreciated by many of those responsible for the official establishment of Catholic Action.

One major reason for their confusion was the haphazard manner in which disconnected elements of Jocist thought arrived in Australia. The doctrine did not arrive in one complete package to facilitate a coherent and thorough understanding of how the different elements of Jocism dovetailed into a complete philosophy of Catholic Action.

Kevin Kelly: Australian Prophet of the Belgian JOC and Specialised Catholic Action

Kevin Kelly was introduced to the Campion Society in late 1931. He threw himself into Campion activities. His intellectual talents and strong personality meant that he became one of its most active and influential members.

Kelly was born in Ballarat on 6 May 1910. His father was consecutively a goods porter, shunter and guard in the Victorian Railways. Kelly's father became deeply involved in the Conscription furore of 1916–17 on the anti-Conscription side while he was president of the Ballarat branch on the Australian Railways Union between 1917 and 1918. He was also involved in the campaign for a wages board for the Victorian Railways. As a result of these agitations he was moved three hundred miles away to Bairnsdale, in Gippsland, in 1918.

Kelly was born into the Catholic Irish-Australian working class as it was about to step onto the federal stage of Australian politics, flexing its muscles through the Australian Labor Party. As a boy, Kelly breathed the atmosphere of political-religious debate in the upper echelons of the Catholic working class. Ever since he was bounced on the knee of close family friend and future Labor Prime Minister, James Scullin, Kelly's social environment had been coloured with questions of religion, economics and politics. How did injustice occur? What

---

5.   Pope Pius XI, Quadragesimo Anno. 1931, 143.

form would a Christian social order take? How could it be built? In what manner could the Catholic Church influence politics?

Believe it or not, living in Bairnsdale was a factor in the history of the YCW in Australia in that Kevin was introduced to French under Mother Athanasius, a French Notre Dame de Sion nun stationed at St Mary's Primary School. This skill would later enable him to access and translate Belgian JOC literature. When the Kellys moved to the Melbourne suburb of Malvern in 1924, the French influence in his education continued at the local De La Salle College of the French-founded De La Salle Brothers. In the local parish of St Joseph, Malvern, served by the French Vincentian order, he had access to the extensive library of American, Irish and English Catholic Truth Society pamphlets, compiled by a Brother Whelan, which also broadened his education and nurtured his developing interest in the problems of transforming an inherently chaotic, pluralist, secular society on the basis of Christian social principles.

After completing his Leaving Certificate in 1927, Kevin Kelly took a temporary job as a teacher at Toorak Central School before taking a position as a clerk in March 1928 in the Neglected Children's Section of the Victorian Chief Secretary's Office. Family poverty had prevented him from pursuing full-time study for a degree in Law so he enrolled in a Bachelor of Arts degree, part-time, at the University of Melbourne. Kelly worked in the Neglected Children's Section until 1936. During that time he came into contact with the most destitute women and children in the state at the time of the worst economic depression in Australia since 1891. His dealings with these sections of society continued when he moved to the head office of the Chief Secretary's Department in 1936 as personal assistant to the Inspector-General of Gaols and Reformatories. Exposure to instances of social injustice continued as secretary to the Royal Commission into the explosion that killed twenty men at the Wonthaggi State Coal Mine in 1937.

Kelly was also a constant contributor and energetic organiser from 1936 of the new *Catholic Worker*, the pages of which reflected his close knowledge of the poorest sections of Victorian society.

In 1932, the founder of the Central Catholic Library in Melbourne, the Jesuit Fr William Hackett, asked Kelly to write an article in French for the French Jesuit review *Dossiers de l'Action Sociale* on the theme of the Socialisation Objective of the ALP.[6]

---

6.   Pope Pius XI, *Quadragesimo Anno*, 1931, 143.

Kelly, a family friend of Scullin, a member of the ALP and a member of the Council of the Public Service Association of Victoria, was well placed to contribute such an article. Payment for the article—published in 1933—was a bundle of books, all in French. Some dealt with Catholic Action in general and others with 'Specialised' Catholic Action. Included in the literature was a copy of *Dossiers de l'Action Sociale* which carried an article on the Jeunesse Ouvriere Chretienne or JOC, the Young Christian Workers. This gift marked the beginning of the promotion of the Jocist understanding of Catholic Action in Australia, though not the full understanding of Jocism itself. But it did lead to Kelly's contact with the Belgian YCW in 1936. Knowledge of the essentials of YCW aims and methods dates from this 1936 contact.

The Catholic Action literature, received in payment for the review article began to influence the intellectual interests of the Campion Society, and from there the policies of the Campion-inspired and staffed Australian National Secretariat of Catholic Action set up in 1937 by the bishops to spread Catholic Action throughout Australia. Although ANSCA was at first influenced more by ideas akin to Italian Catholic Action, as early as April 1934 Kevin Kelly was trying to persuade the Campions of the correctness of the specialised form of Catholic Action and later the Jocist model for this specialised form.

Kelly probably didn't need any encouragement to study the French Catholic Action literature received - note it was not Belgian Jocist literature as yet. Nevertheless, by December 1934, he was ready to accept an invitation, along with the founder of the Adelaide Guild of Social Studies, Paul McGuire, to give the keynote address to the Melbourne University Newman Society's Convention of Catholic University Bodies being held as part of the Melbourne Eucharistic Congress activities. Kelly spoke on the topic 'The Theory of Catholic Action', and McGuire 'The Practice of Catholic Action'.

Kelly based his talk on ideas gleaned from the Parisian review[7] Notebooks on Religious and Social Action. (*Les Cahiers d'Action Religieuse et Sociale.*) From the evidence of Kelly's correspondence to Paul McGuire before the talk, and the talk itself, the idea of Catholic Action he gained from this review was Jocist inspired.[8] The spiritual

---

7. Interview with KTK, 25–28/11/78.
8. Correspondence and notes for 1934 Convention talk in possession of KTK.

goal of forming lay apostles and organising them in specialised organisations, that is, divided by the principle of unique interest, environment or milieu, is present. But the means of this formation—the see, judge, act element—is missing at this point.

Belgium Correspondence, 1936–40

Kelly did not correspond with the JOC in Europe until 1936. In late April of that year he wrote to Europe for more information on Catholic Action, particularly the specialised youth movements. Considering his enthusiasm in 1934, the two year silence is strange. According to Kelly, other commitments prevented him from doing so.[9] Apart from working full-time in the Public Service, he was active in the administration and expansion of the Campion Society. He was Master of the Catholic Evidence Guild, which he had founded with Brian Harkin in 1933. At the University of Melbourne, he had been studying part-time for an arts degree, was involved in the Newman Society and was a member of the university's debating teams. During 1936, he became increasingly involved in the *Catholic Worker*, which had been first published in February of that year by a group of Campions led by BA Santamaria. In between, Kelly had to keep up his reading program provided by the Campion Society. Like many other leading Campions, he had lived several lives by the time he was thirty years of age.

Kelly sent the first letter to Paris, to what he believed to be headquarters of the JOC. The French JOC passed his letter on to international bureau of the Belgian JOC. On May 22 1936 Fr Robert Kothen, ecclesiastical assistant to Joseph Cardijn, replied to Kelly, sending some JOC literature.[10]

Kelly and Kothen corresponded for the next five years until the German Army invaded Belgium in the Spring of 1940. After World War II ended, their friendship and correspondence continued until Fr Kothen's death in 1953. Fr Kothen was the channel through which a more complete notion of the YCW came to Melbourne and, thus, to Australia. Apart from designing and forging the template which

---

9. Interview, 25–28/11/1978
10. Correspondence between K T Kelly and R Kothen, 1936–40, 1945-53, held by KT Kelly at 30 Golden Grove, Canberra, ACT

would later guide the founders of Melbourne YCW, and thus the Australian YCW and other Australian Jocist movements, Joseph Cardijn had no hands-on influence in establishing the pioneer YCW Movement in Australia. The details of YCW doctrine were gleaned from the literature Kothen supplied - not from the letters: Kothen's letters were short and personal; there wasn't any lengthy, complex exposition of the doctrine. He let the official JOC publications speak for themselves.

Between 1936 and 1940, Kelly received, at least, ten books and pamphlets: Of these, Kelly believed the *Manual of JOC*, especially— along with *The Worker-Layman, Catholic Action in the Working-Class, The JOC Faces the Problem of the Young Wage Earner* - to be the correct guidelines for setting up the YCW in Melbourne.[11] Kelly adopted the position of *de facto* ambassador of the JOC in Australia - sending back reports to Brussels on the different Catholic youth movements in Melbourne in the 1930s; and of his own attempts to persuade these movements, ANSCA and the Melbourne Diocesan Secretariat of Catholic Action of the necessity of a movement for young Christian workers run on Jocist lines. He also reported on his attempt to start a YCW group in Oakleigh in 1938 with a local worker, Tom Hogan. Other matters reported on included the struggle between different Melbourne Catholic youth movements to be accepted as the official youth movement of the Archdiocese of Melbourne; and the handing over in the middle of 1939 of the responsibility for founding the YCW in Melbourne to the newly formed Melbourne YCW Priests Committee. (When I researched the history in the late 1970s, there was no evidence that Fr Lombard had any detailed knowledge of YCW methods before early 1939 as there had been no experimenting with Jocism in his parish of Northcote in 1938 in his first year as a priest).

The Belgian literature began to open Kelly's eyes further to the key points in Jocism and the Jocist understanding of Catholic Action. By early 1937, the key point learnt was the division of Catholic Action into two groups – mass movements and groups of militants. Militants were leaders who were active as apostles or were actively forming themselves to be apostles.[12] The 'mass' were those outside the militants who were either passive or indifferent Christians, or non-Chris-

---

11. KTK to Ken Mitchell, 30/6/1939, KTK to R Kothen 13/7/1939, 25/2/1940.
12. Campion Society Memorandum A to Dr Mannix, 1937, 24.

tians; who needed to be worked upon by the militants—the bearers of the Holy Spirit - in order that, respectively, they might be re-activated or activated. By this stage Kelly was also aware that if Catholics were linked together in an organisation which, in its membership, corresponded to some natural social grouping, then the endeavour had a much better chance of survival and success.[13] In other words, the majority of labourers would more readily associate with labourers than with middle class professionals.

If Kelly was not already aware of further details of the Belgian JOC, Paul McGuire's articles in Melbourne's *Advocate* during September and October 1937 certainly supplied him with any remaining information that he needed to evangelise and to attempt to establish the JOC in Melbourne. The broad, apostolic strategy was to penetrate the secular environment by means of groups of committed apostles with a view to re-establishing the Christian basis of Western Civilisation.[14] The means to implement this strategy was the agenda of the militants study circle—prayer, Gospel meditation, report on the preceding week's action, enquiries (see, judge, act) on personal contacts and wider social problems, and then a chaplain's talk and the setting of tasks for the following week. The study circle or leadership group was the vehicle for attaining the formation objective: formation *through* action.[15] However, in 1937, Kelly, like McGuire, lacked a sense of the cohesiveness of Jocist doctrine. His experiences in 1938 educated him further.

In late 1938, Kelly began to realise that the officers of ANSCA were uncritically selecting odd pieces of Jocist doctrine to solve certain problems in other methods of formation without understanding that, because of the cohesiveness of Jocism, the use of elements of Jocism outside of the total body of Jocist understanding and organisation was meaningless and ineffective. The particular centre of dispute between Kelly and ANSCA was the principle of specialisation—apostles of the workers must be the workers, for, by and among themselves.[16] Kelly informed Fr Kothen that the national secretariat was inclined not so much to promote the 'JOC as JOC', but to use the doctrine, method and techniques of the JOC to promote either middle-class organisa-

---

13. Campion Society Memorandum A to Dr Mannix, 1937, 37.
14. Campion Society Memorandum A to Dr Mannix, 1937, 29–31.
15. Campion Society Memorandum A to Dr. Mannix, 1937, 29–31.
16. KTK to RK.30/8/1938.

tions like the Catholic Youth Movement or general movements like the Catholic Young Mens Society, and its youth CYMS Legion.[17]

Kelly suspected that the inaugural Director of ANSCA, Frank Maher, a lawyer and teacher of middle-class origins, did not fully understand the solidarity of working-class consciousness. For example, Maher displayed a classic middle-class presumption when he queried the naming of a worker's movement as such for fear that it would stigmatise the movement.[18] Kelly's perception of Maher's misunderstanding of Jocism as an ideal form of Catholic Action irritated the peaceable director of ANSCA, especially when it was conveyed— to Maher's thinking—in Kelly's vigorous manner of criticism.[19] Also, Kelly had fallen out with the ANSCA vice-director, BA Santamaria, over the National Health and Pensions Insurance Bill 1938.[20] Santamaria's cavalier approach to the subtleties in official Church understandings of the relationship between the Church and State had begun to worry Kelly and other Campions. In correspondence with ANSCA in 1939, Kelly argued strongly that there should be no direct, organisational YCW effort in the unions or in political parties.[21]

ANSCA's eclectic approach to the development of a method for the formation of Catholic Actionists pushed Kelly to see the totality of Jocist doctrine. The final act in his intellectual odyssey to full knowledge of the JOC was to see in 1939 that, as a philosophy of Catholic Action, it was comprehensive and inclusive.[22]

Once he understood that a significant aspect of Jocism was its coherence, Kelly took several steps to maintain this integrity. First, he sought successfully to have ANSCA designate him as the official correspondent of the Belgian JOC in Australia, a position he had held *de facto* since 1936.[23] As official correspondent, Kelly could at least hope to prevent the Belgian JOC recognising any hybrid YCW that ANSCA established. Second, he wanted ANSCA to recognise a com-

---

17. KTK. to RK.8/3/1939.
18. Draft Memorandum on Specialisation, 1939, 6, file 'Specialisation 1' held in the archives of National Civic Council.
19. F K Maher to RK, 9/5/1939.
20. Interview with Ken Mitchell.
21. KTK to FKM, 9/10/1939.
22. Kelly, KT, editor, *Young Christian Workers*, ACTS, 822, 31 July, 1939, 5. Also KTK to RK 13/7/1939.
23. Joseph Cardijn to FKM, 28/4/1939, KTK to RK 8/3/1939.

mittee of those who understood Jocism, the members of which would be responsible for the publication of authentic and sound translations of Joseph Cardijn's works.[24]

The second proposal was never realised but the first—official correspondent—was agreed to on 3 October 1939[25] after representation from Fr Cardijn.[26]

In the third step, Kelly recommended to Ken Mitchell, MDSCA diocesan organiser, that a special committee be formed to assist in the formation, by young workers, of a YCW movement.[27] By means of this committee, he hoped to directly influence the future nature and organisation of the Melbourne and Australian YCW. The documents of the Belgian JOC referred to earlier—*Manual of JOC*, etc, *The Worker-Layman, Catholic Action in the Working-Class, The JOC Faces the Problem of the Young Wage Earner*—were to be regarded as binding on the committee. Subject to the authority of the bishops, this committee would be responsible for the formulation of official Catholic Action policy for the YCW Movement in Melbourne and Australia. It was to arrange classes in YCW doctrine and method and make arrangements for the financing, clerical, editorial and organising work of the movement.[28] Finally, through his friendship with *Advocate* associate editor Fr James Murtagh, Kelly edited the first Australian publication which dealt solely with the YCW—simply entitled *The Young Christian Workers*. The Australian Catholic Truth Society published the pamphlet in July, 1939 and 15,000 copies were sold within six months.[29]

The first two chapters were written by Kevin Kelly. The first, 'Australia and the JOC', set the Catholic Action objective in general: 'If we are to win Australia for Christ and to secure Social Justice, Catholic workers need to know the Faith and understand Australia.'

The third chapter was an article by Cardijn entitled 'The New Paganism'.[30] This article was the first publication of the thought of

---

24. KTK to RK 13/7/1939.
25. FKM to KTK, 3/10/1939.
26. Joseph Cardijn to FKM, 28/4/1939.
27. KTK to Ken Mitchell (KM), 30/6/1939.
28. KTK to KM, 30/6/1939.
29. KTK to RK, 25/2/1940.
30. KTK to RK, 25/2/1940, 7–14.

Cardijn in Australia in the original, but its focus was Catholic Action and not the YCW directly.

The fourth chapter was more specific. Entitled 'The Young Christian Workers Movement', it was penned by Fr Kothen.[31] Affirming the dependence of the YCW on the Church, Fr Kothen pointed to the basis of the YCW in Realism (that is, seeing the true situation of young workers), Idealism (judging by Christian standards) and then Action to restore justice. The final chapter of the pamphlet contained the second and third articles written by Paul McGuire for the *Advocate* in 1937.[32]

The pamphlet contained all the essentials in aims, method and organisation necessary to establish a theoretically correct Young Christian Workers movement. Its publication, occurring three weeks after the institution of the Melbourne YCW Priests Committee, was the final act but one in Kelly's six year career in Melbourne and Australia as prophet of the YCW and Jocist Catholic Action. The last act was when Kelly handed over a large quantity of the Jocist literature to Frs Lombard, Frank Ford, and John F Kelly on 29 March 1940.

His retreat from active involvement in establishing the lay apostolate was made permanent by the outbreak of World War II. By the time his service in naval intelligence in the Pacific had ended six years later, a generation of youth had passed and he was not recognised when he dropped into the YCW building behind St Francis Church. He went on to have a distinguished career in Australia's diplomatic service, rising to become ambassador to Portugal and then Argentina. He maintained a lifelong interest in Catholic intellectual pursuits, in particular promoting the thought of the French philosopher and Catholic layman Jacques Maritain. He died in Canberra in 1994, aged eighty-four, still very proud of his role in bringing the idea of Jocism and specialised Catholic Action to Australia, and so he should have been.

---

31. KTK to RK, 25/2/1940, 15–24.
32. *YCW*, pp24-33.

Archbishop Justin Simonds and the YCW

Max Vodola

Justin Daniel Simonds was born on 22 May 1890 in the small hamlet of Stonehenge, a few kilometres south of Glen Innes in northern New South Wales.[1] He was the youngest child of Peter and Catherine Simonds. Justin's father was a senior teacher then principal with the Department of Public Instruction. While the four Simonds boys received a thoroughly Catholic formation at home, they were educated in the state system. Justin undertook seminary studies at St Patrick's College, Manly, and was ordained a priest in 1912. After only one year as an assistant priest in the parish of Bega, Simonds returned to Manly (then Springwood) to lecture in Sacred Scripture, Greek and Philosophy until 1927. In 1928, he was sent to Louvain to complete a doctorate in philosophy. While many historians hold strongly to John Molony's thesis[2] regarding the Irish-born/Roman-trained characteristics of many in the Australia hierarchy, Justin Simonds was certainly not in this mould!

It was during this time in Louvain that Simonds was exposed to the Catholic intellectual climate of Europe, particularly the development of Catholic Action and the Young Christian Workers (YCW), Cardijn of course having studied at Louvain himself.[3] According to Simonds, 'I happened to be in Belgium during some of the period when the J.O.C was being organized by its founder, Canon Cardijn,

---

1. Max Vodola, *Simonds: A Rewarding Life* (East Melbourne, Vic: Catholic Education Office, 1997).
2. John Molony, *The Roman Mould of the Australian Catholic Church* (Melbourne: Melbourne University Press, 1969).
3. Marguerite Fievez and Jacques Meert, *Cardijn* translated by E. Mitchinson (London: Young Christian Workers, 1974).

and know something of the problem it was created to solve and the methods employed with such success'.[4]

National Episcopal Chairman

There is no need for me to revisit the history of the Campion Society, Catholic Action and the YCW in Australia as most of you are familiar with this chronological sequence. The bishops decided in 1937 to establish the Australian National Secretariat of Catholic Action (ANSCA) as the umbrella organization to coordinate the various strands of Catholic Action. In 1936, Justin Simonds was appointed the Archbishop of Hobart and remained there for only five years. Soon after his arrival in Hobart, Simonds published a pastoral letter on 'Our Incorporation In The Priesthood of Jesus Christ'. Simonds had just celebrated his silver jubilee of priestly ordination. Whilst recalling in the document the dignity and importance of the Catholic priesthood, Simonds addressed the laity in a quite radical and remarkable way. He reminded them of their sharing in the priesthood of Christ by virtue of baptism and went on to explain at great length the importance of baptism in the sacramental life of the Church. Simonds called on the laity to be conscious of their active sharing in the celebration of Mass, rather than being mere spectators at a religious ceremony. At the end of the pastoral letter, Simonds recalled that the practical application of doctrinal truth was directed towards the duty of organizing the laity in the work of Catholic Action. 'The supreme aim of Catholic Action is to bring the principles of Christ to bear upon every phase of our personal and social life'.[5] It was a principle that guided Archbishop Justin Simonds throughout his life.

In 1942, in the middle of the Second World War, Simonds was transferred to Melbourne as Coadjutor Archbishop to Daniel Mannix. The circumstances and consequences of that transfer are a matter of historical record.[6] In 1943 Simonds was appointed National Episcopal Chairman of the YCW. In his first major address, Simonds makes a number of salient and prescient points that with the passage

4. Archbishop Justin Simonds, 'Young Christian Workers: First Address of Episcopal Chairman, Most Rev J Simonds, DD, To YCW Chaplains on the Policy of the Movement in Australia' (Melbourne, Vic: YCW/The Advocate Press, 1943)
5. Vodola, *Simonds: A Rewarding Life*, 36.
6. Vodola, *Simonds: A Rewarding Life*.

of time deserve much closer attention. On why Catholic Action and the Jocists were established, Simonds stated:

> It has been stated on reliable authority that nine-tenths of the Belgian boys and girls, who began their industrial life at the age of fourteen in factories and workshops, abandoned all religious practice, and were lost to the Church within a few months. The figures seem incredible, but it is admitted by those in close touch with the industrial youth of Belgium that they are not exaggerated.[7]

Simonds clearly articulates the reality of the de-Christianization and rapid secularization of Europe that was occurring throughout the first part of the twentieth century which, as we know, was the continual manifestation of the effects of the Industrial Revolution. The vision of Cardijn and the YCW was to help address this rapidly changing social, cultural, political and economic milieu in terms of the ultimate impact on parish life and in the Catholic formation of the young. Cardijn wanted a thorough Christian formation of the young worker that was religious, intellectual, social, vocational and moral. The YCW was seeking to address the issue of the inter-face between faith and culture and the unique place of the lay vocation in the life of the Church long before the Second Vatican Council.

In terms of seeing the correlation between Belgium and Australia, Simonds stated:

> Since most of these children spent six to eight years in the Catholic schools, the strength of materialistic socialism in Belgian industrial life was recognized as the greatest challenge to the Catholic life of Belgium. Though the problem in Australia may not be so appalling, yet everyone in touch with youth knows very well that the defections of our Catholic youth in the post-school age reach depressing proportions. The number of boys who have never been to the Sacraments since they left school is far too large …[8]

This analysis of the Catholic situation in Australia should eliminate forever the notion that somehow the Second Vatican Council was

---

7. Simonds, 'Young Christian Workers: First Address of Episcopal Chairman', 1943.
8. Simonds, 'Young Christian Workers: First Address of Episcopal Chairman', 1943.

responsible for the rapid decline in vocations, a significant drop in Mass attendance and the loss of a major proportion of post-secondary Catholic youth. In fact, Vatican II was using the methodology of Cardijn and the YCW to help renew Catholic theology in the face of the rapidly changing cultural landscape of post-war Europe. While Catholic schools, seminaries and convents in Australia were literally bursting at the seams at this time, it was really masking a more brutal and confronting sociological and cultural reality for the Church which required both a new language and new theological method. Fighting secularism and materialism from the trenches of the firmly established Irish-Catholic ghetto in Australia was now a thing of the past.

In 1943 Simonds was firmly committed to the YCW method of 'see, judge and act' and Cardijn's determination for a well formed, mature and articulate laity in the Church. Simonds wanted a laity that truly honoured the grace and dignity that came to them from the sacraments of Baptism and Confirmation and not to act in the Church and world as poor imitators of the vocation to priesthood and the religious life. The present writer, in Church history lectures at Catholic Theological College East Melbourne, always introduces students to the powerful and compelling rhetoric of Canon Joseph Cardijn that formed generations of lay leaders in Australia and throughout the Catholic world:

> It is not your business to imitate priests and religious. You are lay people, young workers, engaged couples, tomorrow, fathers, wives, mothers. The worker's tools stand in his hand as the chalice and paten in the hands of the priest…It is not a question in the factory of having a rosary or missal in one's hands. In the factory the tools of the job are in one's hands. You have to work; but you have to also learn a spirituality in which one's work becomes one's prayer.[9]

According to Simonds, the YCW was 'the finest example of the Church's apostolate amongst the workers that has yet been evolved'.

Political Complications

As the YCW grew and prospered in Australia, Simonds was increasingly at odds with Mannix and Santamaria in terms of the Move-

---

9.   Vodola, *Simonds: A Rewarding Life*, 13.

ment and the overtly political manner of transforming the temporal order which lay at the heart of the colossal industrial and political battles of the Australian Labor Party in the 1950s. Simonds always maintained a 'classic' view of Catholic Action and the YCW that stood above political intrigue and sectarian issues of the day. His private reservations soon became public and revealed serious divisions within the Church, especially among the bishops. At the installation of his friend Eris O'Brien as Archbishop of Canberra and Goulburn in 1954, Simonds stated:

> I am sure that he (O'Brien) will set his face sternly against any attempt to involve the Church in underground political intrigue. Anything of that nature is completely foreign to his character, and he is too well versed in history to imagine that the Church's divine apostolate gains any permanent fruit when any of her misguided children seek to capture political power in her name.[10]

In a 1958 Christmas message on television, which was later published in the *Herald*, Simonds unambiguously attempted to remove himself from public political wrangling:

> . . . since a great number of people have expressed to me their distress that last month, during the election campaign, the Church became involved in bitter political controversy, which is always a regrettable circumstance . . . I am happy to say that I was completely unconnected with it altogether . . . Whenever the Church's ministry and spiritual mission becomes befogged with political issues the cause of religion always suffers.[11]

Despite the bitterness, division and public wrangling concerning the Church, the Movement and the Labor Split of 1955, Catholic Action and the YCW in Australia planted rich and fertile seeds that would come to fruition at Vatican II. Long before the Second Vatican Council, laity and clergy in Australia were formed in a spirit that oriented them towards the Gospel call to social justice, the unique and indispensable place of the lay vocation and lay leadership in the life of the Church, an authentic lay spirituality based fundamentally on the

---

10. Vodola, *Simonds: A Rewarding Life*, 77.
11. Vodola, *Simonds: A Rewarding Life*, 81.

dignity and grace of Baptism and Confirmation, the transformation of the temporal order on the basis of 'see, judge and act' and active participation in the sacramental life of the community of faith.[12] The Council documents are replete with these themes. Whilst Simonds attended every session of the Council and was quick to begin implementing the liturgical reforms, his potentially significant contribution was compromised by poor health and failing eyesight. The late Bishop Joseph O'Connell, a curate at St Mary's West Melbourne during Simonds' tenure as parish priest and coadjutor-archbishop, recalls reading the Latin documents of the Council to Simonds because of his failing eyesight.[13]

The Catholic Church in Australia owes Archbishop Justin Simonds a great debt of gratitude for his encouragement of the YCW and his commitment to a well formed and articulate laity who genuinely lived out their Christian vocation in the world. So much of this rich theology and practical application was alive in the Church long before Vatican II in terms of dealing with the rapidly changing social, cultural, religious and political landscape of post-war Europe.

12. *Vatican Council II: Constitutions, Decrees and Declarations,* edited by Austin Flannery (Northport, New York: Costello Publishing Company, 1996).
13. Vodola, *Simonds: A Rewarding Life,* 85.

Fr Frank Lombard (1910–1967)

Bruce Duncan CSsR

Frank Lombard was born in Brighton Victoria on 24 April 1911, the youngest of five children and third son of John Lombard, member of Victorian police and Bridget (nee Collins), who had emigrated from Ireland in the 1880s. Frank spent his childhood at Brighton and Berwick before his father a policeman, moved to Ivanhoe police station. Lack of formal education prevented him rising above senior constable in his thirty years of service, and reinforced in him the desire to provide a good education for his children.

Frank attended the State Primary school at Berwick, then Parade Christian Brothers in Melbourne to the Leaving Certificate. He completed Matriculation at the new St Kevin's Christian Brothers College in Toorak. Though his marks were above average, he inclined rather to sport.

His family was strongly religious, especially his mother, and his father had three sisters enter religious life. After a retreat in 1927 at the seminary at Werribee, Frank decided to become a priest. He returned to St Kevin's to study Latin, during which time his mother died.

In the seminary he gained a reputation for being not too bright and was the butt of jokes. However, he grew to 6'2" and 17 stone; he had a splendid physique and ability in football, tennis, athletics and especially swimming. However, he caught tuberculosis in 1933 and had to spend twelve months in the Greenvale Sanatorium in Melbourne. After his return to the Werribee seminary in 1934, he was ordained by Archbishop Mannix on 26 July 1936 at St Patrick's Cathedral, Melbourne.

From his first posting in 1937 to Northcote parish he developed a keen interest in youth. Within a few months he had formed study circles for the Catholic Young Men's Society, which catered for young working men over the age of 20.[1]

During 1938 he was inspired to combine the spiritual drive of Catholic Action for youth with the natural energy of youth sporting activities. As chaplain to a boys club which played football in the Catholic Boys' Legion competition, he considered first setting up a junior section to the Holy Name Society to encourage monthly communion. Within a year, he had nearly 200 male youth enrolled in the parish junior section of the Holy Name.

During the first half of 1939, Lombard learned more about YCW principles from some current literature, but especially Kevin T. Kelly's pamphlet, *Young Christian Workers* of July 1939. He did not consider himself a scholar, but he had a unique ability to translate ideas into the Australian cultural context, so he began to see how the ideas of Canon Cardijn could be used.

In July 1939, a priests' committee was formed to develop YCW in Australia, with the encouragement of BA Santamaria, at that time assistant director of the Australian National Secretariat for Catholic Action (ANSCA). In March 1940, Kevin Kelly relinquished to the committee his role as official correspondent with the Belgian authorities of YCW. Kelly had had himself named as correspondent because of disagreements with ANSCA about the role of Catholic Action, and the priests' committee too was to be jealous of its independence.

The YCW employed what it called the 'see, judge, act' method that had been developed by Cardijn, and aimed to help young workers internalise Catholic religious values and to apply them in their work situation, to draw others to the faith, combat exploitation and improve working conditions. After discussing a short passage from the Gospel, with the guidance of a prepared leader, each small group would then evaluate the members' life or work situation in the light of the Gospel and determine on some action to change the situation for the better. At their next meeting, members would discuss and evaluate their action, and repeat the process. Thus the process was geared to encourage youth to use their own judgment and to take action

---

1. David Kehoe, Draft history of the YCW in Melbourne, Chapter 4: 'A Priest', (Melbourne: Melbourne YCW archives), 1–3.

on their own initiative after evaluating evidence, called an enquiry, which could be on any topic. However, party-political activity was rigorously excluded.

Much of this social focus in Cardijn had to be modified in Melbourne because of the Second World War and because Lombard's initial effort was to attract all youth into Catholic social activities, football or learn-to-dance classes, as a means to reinforce religious practice.

Archbishop Mannix appointed Lombard an army chaplain in March 1940 on three-monthly tours of duty and he was away from his parish groups during the following year. Santamaria wrote a pamphlet, *How to start the JOC*,[2] in March 1940, drawing on Belgian sources, but the priests' committee preferred their own literature and that of Kevin Kelly. In mid-1940, Mannix appointed Lombard the YCW Melbourne chaplain, outside the control of ANSCA. Lombard expanded his groups in October 1940 to take over the Catholic Boys' Legion which became YCW in September 1941. By this time, the strong-willed Lombard was unwilling to have YCW come under the control of ANSCA or to follow its direction.

Lombard was appointed curate at Collingwood in September 1942 to give him more time to move about the archdiocese, and the following September, Archbishop Justin Simonds, the new coadjutor to Mannix, was appointed bishop in charge of national YCW which had been established earlier in the year. Against ANSCA, Simonds strongly supported Lombard's views about the independence of YCW.[3]

Not only did Lombard have a remarkable charisma for working with youth, he was a splendid public speaker, especially to large crowds, like the Catholic Action rallies at Xavier College, Kew, which attracted crowds of 20,000 for the 1942 rally, 30,000 in 1943, and between these two figures till 1949 when they were discontinued. The youth sections numbered from 5000 (in 1944) to 12,000 (in 1945). These rallies were a feast of Catholic militancy, with flags, marching displays, sporting events and religious services.

---

2. The JOC were the French initials for the YCW, Young Christian Workers' Movement in English. The members were at times referred to as Jocists.
3. Kehoe, Draft History, 'Military Service', 64ff.

The YCW expanded rapidly in 1943 to 47 groups by October 1943, numbering 4,000 members in Melbourne. It ran learn-to-dance classes, savings schemes and sporting activities. In 1943 it had fifty-one football teams and thirty-eight cricket teams, as well as offering swimming, athletics and boxing.[4] Its newspaper, *New Youth*, became monthly from June 1944.

YCW reached its high point in 1947, with 3,300 members in Melbourne, 18 per cent of the Catholic age cohort at the time, and extending services to fifty-five per cent of the age group. But by 1951 increasing social mobility helped reduce Melbourne membership to 1400, though parish organisation was strengthened again by 1954, when its membership was only 875 in forty-seven parishes.

The YCW introduced housing schemes and helped promote legislation allowing housing co-operatives in Victoria in 1944.[5] Between 1945 and 1960, YCW sponsored twenty housing co-operatives which financed 2600 homes. Co-operative housing societies in general in Victoria helped people buy 37,000 homes. It also promoted trading co-operatives from 1949, which by 1961 had 2600 members and sales of more than one million pounds.[6] From 1956, the YCW promoted parish credit societies, and formed a Co-operative Permanent Building Society in 1957. From 1952, YCW also offered an insurance service. It ran a youth training centre, 'Maiya Wamba' (aboriginal for House of Youth) in Cheltenham, and established a Men's Extension Committee to raise funds (this later became YCW Holdings Melbourne).

Fr Lombard became strongly opposed to BA Santamaria's Movement. Fr James McInerney had been transferred by Mannix from an air force chaplaincy to establish Catholic Action groups in factories in Melbourne. As one of the two ecclesiastical assistants to ANSCA, McInerney hoped to draw on the YCW membership for leaders for these factory groups engaged in the struggle against the communists, but by mid-1944 YCW was distrustful of the Santamaria Movement. Santamaria had to defend his conception of Catholic Action to Archbishop Simonds who feared that ANSCA was taking YCW in a wrong

---

4.   Kehoe, Draft History, Chapter 4: 'A Priest', 90.

5.   Kehoe, Chapter 7: 'To educate, serve and represent: the family', 46–7.

6.   Ted Long, *Helping each other through co-operatives*, Melbourne: ACTS pamphlet, 10 January 1962, 5–6.

direction; in June 1944 Simonds argued that Catholic Action had to change social and economic conditions.[7]

In July 1945, the lay secretary of the YCW, Frank McCann, put to Archbishop Simonds Santamaria's plan 'for what the YCW regarded as an official link with the trade unionists'. Simonds rejected any official link.

After the Catholic bishops approved the formation of the Catholic Social Studies Movement (CSSM) in September 1945, the YCW priests' committee delegated Fr Lombard and Fr G. Coghlan to discuss with Santamaria co-operation against communism. As YCW included young male workers up to the age of twenty-five, Santamaria saw them as a natural base for trained and motivated recruits for his Movement, but did not want the YCW setting up groups in factories which could complicate the work of the Movement or lead Catholics in another direction. Lombard did not join these discussions.

Santamaria made a second approach to the YCW in October–November 1945, proposing combined committees of his Movement and YCW members to fight communism in the unions. Lombard did not want to see YCW become preoccupied with the communist issue and, with the support of Simonds and the priests' committee, declined. Simonds did not want the YCW to be politically involved or swamped by older men, but he allowed a loose association and individuals to become involved.

The disagreement was referred to Mannix, with Lombard determined to hold his ground even if it cost him his parish. When Mannix did not appear to make a decision, Lombard asked him what would happen to the YCW if it did not carry out the Archbishop's command. Mannix replied that he had not commanded anything but expected Lombard to interpret his wishes. According to David Kehoe, in 'great trepidation, Fr Lombard stuck to his decision. But the archbishop did not order the YCW to co-operate with the CSSM on Mr Santamaria's terms', and continued to support the YCW publicly.[8]

Santamaria again approached the YCW after the 1946 Easter conference of the ALP, but was again rebuffed. Instead he turned to the Catholic Young Men's Organisation which was not a Catholic Action body and hence not so concerned about being non-political.

---

7. Santamaria to Simonds, 28 June 1944.
8. David Kehoe, Draft history of the YCW, Chapter 8: 'Work', 67.

However, as he was about to go overseas, Simonds wrote to Santamaria concerned about serious conflict between ANSCA and executives of the Catholic Action bodies, particularly that these were not to become involved in the political work of the CSSM, as the YCW was not restricted to being a 'a mere parish society, as you suggest . . .' He nominated Fr Lombard as one of the YCW representatives, and insisted that Catholic Action was not under the control of any other organisation.[9] However, the Episcopal Committee for Catholic Action said that YCW for the time being was not to develop factory or 'locational' groups, but remain with parish ones.[10]

Lombard continued to push strongly for the independence of YCW from ANSCA, and at a conference of priests in September 'clashed repeatedly' with Santamaria, with Lombard wanting the priests' committee to assume control.[11] Santamaria wrote to Mannix that three times he had visited Lombard only to be rebuffed. YCW refused to accept the co-ordination of ANSCA.[12] The Episcopal Committee said the priests could form an advisory committee, but the co-ordinating role was to be done by ANSCA.[13]

In January 1947, Simonds wrote to Santamaria about the 'politicising' of Catholic Action and competition between the Movement and the YCW. Santamaria rejected charges of 'dictatorship' over Catholic Action and held his ground.[14] At the next Episcopal Committee meeting, however, Simonds had ANSCA'S co-ordinating role reduced to an advisory one, with final authority lying with the bishop in charge of each movement.[15]

Having secured the independence of the YCW from Santamaria's Movement (CSSM) and ANSCA, the friction between Lombard and Santamaria did not lessen. There was no great difference about

---

9. Simonds to Santamaria, 29 March 1946.
10. Minutes of the seventh meeting of the Episcopal Committee on Catholic Action, Melbourne, 29 April 1946.
11. Gerard Henderson, *Mr Santamaria and the bishops* (Sydney: Studies in the Christian Movement, 1982), 31.
12. Santamaria to Mannix, 1 October 1946.
13. Minutes of the Episcopal Committee on Catholic Action, eighth meeting, 24 October 1946.
14. Andrew Campbell, Politics as a vocation: a critical examination of BA Santamaria and the politics of commitment 1936–57, PhD, School of Social Sciences, Deakin University, 1989, 90.
15. Santamaria, *Daniel Mannix*, 195–6.

current Catholic ideology in general. The YCW shared many of the ANSCA ideas, and was also concerned about communism, but only in the first half of 1944 did it run a national enquiry on communism, and while encouraging members to belong to their unions, only half in fact did so. The YCW saw communism as one urgent issue among others, and did not give it its top priority as did the CSSM.

Lombard and other Catholic Action chaplains strongly objected to Santamaria's dual position as head of Catholic Action from late 1945 and of the political CSSM, and his repeated efforts to co-opt the resources of Catholic Action into the anti-communist fight. In addition, the YCW method encouraged the independence of workers and did not agree with the Leninist model of the CSSM under tight centralised control.

Sharing the same building, the conflict between two views of Catholic Action continued. Santamaria wrote to Mannix on 28 November 1948 offering to resign. He thought the approach of individual charity supported by Fr Charlie Mayne, Ken Mitchell and others doomed to failure; he argued for reform of institutions, with 'large scale action on legislative, political, economic and cultural lines'. Santamaria wanted YCW, the National Catholic Girls Movement (NCGM) and the Melbourne Secretariat of Catholic Action moved to another building, and that Mannix personally direct the secretaries and chaplains to follow ANSCA policy.[16]

However, Mannix did not move against Lombard, and could not do so against Simonds. The Episcopal Committee in March 1949 reiterated ANSCA's 'final authority in all that pertains to the finances and the administration of all the Movements'.[17] Santamaria's definitive move was to have the bishops approve a special statement in early 1950, *Catholic Action in Australia*,[18] demanding the allegiance of all Catholics to Catholic Action and reinforcing the authority of ANSCA over the Movements. While excluding party politics, Catholic Action was not just concerned with individual apostolates, but concerned to create social and cultural forces favourable to Christianity. One of its

---

16. Santamaria to Mannix, 28 November 1948.
17. Minutes of the thirteenth meeting of the Episcopal Committee on Catholic Action, 15 March 1949.
18. *Catholic Action in Australia: Official Statement of the Archbishops and Bishops of Australia Associated in the National Organisation of Catholic Action* [Melbourne, 1950], 3.

objectives was to prepare apostles for the work in trade unions and in rural reform especially.[19]

Meanwhile, in September 1949 Lombard had gone to England and Europe as a ship migrant chaplain at government expense to expedite the dispatch of young British migrants to Australia. On 17 March 1950 he secured government agreement for the migrants to come to Australia. Over the five years till January 1955, YCW was to bring out and help settle 150 migrants, especially through their migrant hostel at Hawthorn.[20] While in Europe, Lombard investigated the YCW in England, France, Belgium, Italy, Germany and Switzerland, and met Cardijn and other YCW leaders. This visit confirmed his view that the Australian YCW had made the right decision to try to influence the mass of workers and not just the leaders.[21]

Lombard in 1950 objected to Simonds to reports that Santamaria wanted to appoint either WE Crowe or John Maynes to be assistant secretary of ANSCA, and instead suggested the YCW's Ted Long for the position.

The YCW especially resented the CSSM getting the lion's share of Church funds. The priests' committee stated in mid-1952 that while the national Catholic Action movements received only £250 each, £7000 went to the CSSM. While entire Catholic Action in Australia received only £5000, part of even this subsidised the CSSM because it paid Santamaria's salary. The CSSM had expanded its staff to 30 full-time people at 252 Swanston Street, but YCW and the NCGM had to cut their staff in half and reduce salaries to the minimum. Moreover, three priests worked full-time for the CSSM, and Catholics had the impression that the CSSM had superseded Catholic Action. Simonds put the YCW case to the bishops who increased funding for 1953 to £500.[22]

The priests' committee in 1952 also objected to the Movement attempting to conquer political parties and its general political activities which were rousing sectarianism against Catholic Action.

Santamaria complained to Mannix in November 1952 about the 'process of attrition' against the Movement and the hostility of YCW which had hindered CSSM recruitment.[23]

---

19. *Catholic Action in Australia*, 18.
20. Kehoe, Chapter 10: 'A new Australia and a new world', 9–10.
21. Kehoe, Chapter 8: 'Work', 3.
22. Kehoe, 'Military Service', 74.
23. Santamaria to Mannix, 11 December 1952.

Amid mounting acrimony in the Catholic Action movements, in October 1953 the Catholic Action chaplains asked the bishops to separate the CSSM from Catholic Action. Under increasing pressure and an increasingly public conflict with the Catholic Action movements, Santamaria proposed the separation of his Movement from Catholic Action, but he would remain secretary of the National Catholic Rural Movement and retain control over the annual social justice statements.[24]

Lombard was irate at Santamaria's letter impugning his obedience to the bishops, and strongly contested his arguments.[25] The Episcopal Committee for Catholic Action itself divided bitterly on the issue, Mannix, Henschke and O'Collins wanting to maintain the current arrangement, and Simonds, Beovich, Toohey and presumably Duhig were opposed. Mannix refused to allow a motion separating the two organisations, to the intense dissatisfaction of Simonds.[26] Simonds made public his dissent at Archbishop Eris O'Brien's installation in Canberra/Goulburn, when he said in his address that O'Brien would 'set his face sternly against any attempt to involve the Church in underground political intrigue.'[27]

The annual meeting of the bishops on 28–29 April 1954 was finally forced to act on the disputes within Catholic Action. Santamaria argued his case strongly, modifying slightly his 'Religious apostolate and political action' speech, arguing that the Movement may have pioneered a new method of Catholic political organisation for other democracies.[28] However, the bishops ruled against Santamaria, who rescued as much as he could by separating the youth movements but not the National Catholic Rural Movement or the social justice statements. In March 1954, the CSSM offices moved from ANSCA to Gertrude Street Fitzroy, and in April 1954 ANSCA closed down.

In 1954 Lombard for health reasons retired as YCW chaplain. However, at his farewell from YCW, the diocesan seminarians booed

24. Santamaria to Episcopal Committee, [n.d.] in YCW file, MAA.
25. Lombard to Episcopal Committee, [before 17 November 1953], in YCW file, MAA.
26. Minutes of the 20th meeting of the Episcopal Committee on Catholic Action, 17 November 1953, MAA.
27. *Catholic weekly*, 7 January 1954, 3.
28. [Santamaria], Observations on the principles of action of the Organisation, April 1954.

him and his close friend and deputy leader of the Australian Labor Party, Arthur Calwell, who was also speaking of Lombard's contribution.[29] Lombard was appointed parish priest of Clayton in January 1955,[30] a parish of 1800 families. He worked energetically to develop a lively community and build thirteen classrooms, a hall and additions to the convent, a presbytery and a church.[31]

Lombard suffered a severe heart attack in 1960, and remained in hospital from March to December 1960 only to be totally invalided for the next seven years. He died of a stroke at Clayton on 28 July 1967 at the age of 56, just three days after his hero Cardijn died in Belgium. Lombard was buried in Melbourne General Cemetery.

Dedicated to young workers and middle-class youth, Lombard's primary emphasis was on the active and intelligent practice of Catholicism. He was tough, determined and strong willed, and some found him authoritarian and difficult to work with; but most admired his manly example of personal discipline and dedication. Critics thought he gave too much emphasis to sport, but it proved an effective way to enthuse and interest youth. Personally he was very frugal and a humble man despite the limelight. According to Bishop John Kelly, 'he under-estimated his own very considerable, intellectual abilities', but compensated for this by his remarkable leadership abilities.[32]

Note on Sources

Most of the YCW records have been lost, but are summarised in David Kehoe's draft history of the YCW in Melbourne (1982–83). Records consulted: the YCW records at Phillip Island, as also the Melbourne Archdiocesan Archives (MAA). Much more detail on the YCW and the CSSM is contained in my *Crusade or Conspiracy: Catholics and the Anti-communist Struggle in Australia* (Sydney: UNSW Press, 2001).

---

29. Bruce Duncan, Interview with Bill Cassidy, YCW youth camp, Phillip Island, 5 July 1995.

30. EJ Long, 'Father Lombard's contribution to the Church in Australia', *Advocate*, 17 August 1967.

31. JJ McLean, 'Fr Lombard looks forward to "great day"', *Advocate*, undated cutting, after May 1967.

32. Bishop Kelly [Melbourne], Comments on David Kehoe's draft history of the YCW, 6 May 1984, in YCW papers, Phillip Island.

Interviewees: Fr Lombard's only remaining sibling, his sister, Lena Murphy; YCW workers Frank McCann and Ted Long; Fr Lombard's housekeeper, Mrs Winifred McCusker; Lombard's curate at Collingwood, Fr Jack Brosnan; and colleagues Fr Charlie McCann (Temples to we, Vic.) and Fr Kevin Toomey (retired, Mt Eliza Vic.).

The following agreed to read the draft this article on Lombard for comment: Frs Toomey, Brosnan and Charlie McCann; Ted Long and Frank McCann; and St Helen Lombard (Frank's niece).

John Neylon Molony (1927–)

Peter Price

In late 2002 I went to Ballarat to begin the eighteen-month prepara-
tory work towards a Diocesan Assembly to be held in May 2004. It
was an intense process of consultation with the People, the Clergy,
the Religious, anybody engaged in the life of the Diocese. I was using
a simple three-question model to spark conversation from all the
groups. My first question was 'What is your strongest memory of
being Catholic in this Diocese?' It was a question designed to bring
out what people treasured most about being Catholic in their Parish within the Diocese.[1] One of my most rewarding engagements was
with the clergy. When I met with them, at Bishop Peter Connors' invitation and asked them that question, there was no hesitation. Almost
unanimously and powerfully, they remembered the experience of
YCW in the Diocese, both as members, and later as Chaplains. For
them 'See, Judge and Act' was something more than a simple thinking system devised by one of the greatest champions of the Lay Apostolate, Joseph Cardinal Cardijn. It was the way of being Catholic in
a world which we are called to transform in the light of the Gospel.

From those conversations it also emerged that one of the key influences on the Ballarat experience and its strong culture of apostolic
action, was John Neylon Molony, Priest of the Diocese of Ballarat, Lay
Apostolate Director, and later revered Historian with a remarkable
academic career, now Emeritus Professor of the Australian National

---

1. The other two questions were: 'What do you see happening around you that gives
you cause for hope, and/or cause for concern?' And, 'How would you describe
your ideal for the future life of the Diocese?' The Assembly process concluded
with a 350-strong gathering in May 2004 that came together without a pre-set
agenda. The agenda came for the floor of the Assembly!

University. But my story today is not about John Molony the Historian. It is about John Molony, apostle and formator of apostles that is my focus this morning. I have a brief fifteen minutes to open up to you a man I have never met, but have admired from a distance over several years. For this brief study, I am working mostly from his own memories written into the first two volumes of his Autobiography, *Luther's Pine* and *By Wendouree*. After a brief survey of John Molony's life, I want to explore the core influences on his commitment to the Lay Apostolate and in particular the YCW.

John Neylon Molony was born on 15 April 1927 at St Kilda, son of Mick Molony and Janie McInerney (whose mother's maiden name was Neylon) of Sea Lake in Victoria's Mallee, about 330 Kilometres from Melbourne. The family moved to Melbourne in 1935 having been forced off the land by drought, recession and low commodity prices. Mick eventually took a job as a truck-driver for the Australian-owned Petrol Company Alba Petroleum (a company unfamiliar to us in these times). They moved around a bit, but finally settled in Williamstown until 1949, when they moved to Buangor in the Western District to run a Pub and farm a couple of small parcels of land. By this time John was in the Seminary of Propaganda Fide in Rome.

After completing High School as a boarder at St Patrick's College Ballarat, John had entered Corpus Christi College Werribee in 1945 at the age of 17. His Bishop O'Collins sent him to Propaganda Fide to complete his studies in August of 1947. He travelled by ship with two other Rome-bound students, Bede Heather (who would later teach me Greek at Springwood, and even later become Bishop of Parramatta), and Frank Little, whom as we all know became Archbishop of Melbourne and is now deceased. John and his companions arrived in Rome on 5 October 1947.

John was ordained in Rome on 21 December 1950 by special Papal privilege, having had his ordination date advanced to enable him to be ordained during the Holy Year of 1950. He celebrated his first Mass the following day with his friend Frank Little alongside him assisting. Among other friends in Rome was Geoff Lloyd, a priest of Canberra/Goulburn Archdiocese. Geoff would later become Diocesan Director of YCW during my days as a YCW Chaplain in that Diocese. He too burned with a strong commitment to the apostolate from his contact with the Cardijn movement during his Roman sojourn.

John Molony spent a further two years in Rome studying for higher degrees in Theology and Canon Law, returning home by sea in early 1954, before taking up his role as Assistant Priest at Ballarat Cathedral. Bishops seemed in those days (and perhaps even still now) to have a penchant for developing Canon Lawyers in their Dioceses, probably in some hope of protection. It has not worked especially well for them.

By 1958, when Cardijn visited Ballarat, John was Director of Catholic Action Youth Movements, and YCW Chaplain, positions he had held almost immediately upon his return. From 1965 onwards, he was laicised, married, completed his MA and PhD in History, and became one of the most prestigious historians in Australia. He was the historian commissioned to write our Bicentennial History.[2] And so we come to my focus for this morning. What moved John Neylon Molony to what he at least implies in his autobiography as a life-long commitment to the Lay Apostolate? I have discerned four major influences.

Influence One: Charlie Mayne SJ

As a young man entering the Seminary, perhaps as most of us did, with ideals of serving the People of God, the foremost influence on him was Jesuit priest, Charlie Mayne. At Werribee in 1945 John came under the influence of one of the great promoters of the Laity, Charlie Mayne SJ, the roll-your-own smoking Dean of Discipline (and later Rector). As Molony wrote in his autobiography, 'Charlie Mayne had the most decisive priestly influence on my life.'[3] So many other Victorian clergy also attest to this influence on them. If you go into the Mannix Library here in Melbourne and browse in the section on Lay Apostolate, ninety percent or more of the books there will carry Charlie Mayne's nameplate on the inside cover. Mayne incidentally seems to have been suspicious of the Santamaria Movement as the 'Enemy of Catholic Action', rather than its champion. Santamaria would later come into Molony's life as well, but I leave others to tell that story.

---

2. Published in Melbourne by Viking Press (Penguin Books Australia), in 1987.
3. Luther's Pine, 130.

Influence Two: Immersion in the Apostolate

The second key influence was his work after ordination among the poorer areas of the Diocese of Rome, as he described it 'working in the Pope's Diocese'. Certainly in 1951 he worked in the Roman *Campagna* Parishes of the Agro Romano district, picked up and driven there in the back of an old truck by a 'young man from *Italian Catholic Action*', called Lello Alberici, a man who would become a lifelong friend. Several readings on John Molony suggest that by the time he left Rome in 1953 he had been formed in his sense of mission by working among the poor of the Agro Romano and among those who were displaced by the upheaval of World War II, living under the broken arches of aqueducts bordering the city, at a place called Quadraro. It was here that he experienced the fundamental mission of the Church, Solidarity with the Poor, the meaning of compassion without judgment, and how to inspire hope even in the direst of circumstances. As he wrote in *By Wendouree*, 'The main thing that distressed me in those early years of my priesthood was not sin but poverty'. Through Lello and his companions, Molony also became aware of the chaotic struggles that characterised Italian Catholic Action at that time.[4]

Influence Three: The 1951 World Congress of Laity

Perhaps the third key influence, again in that year 1951, was his attendance at the first Congress of the Lay Apostolate in Rome in October. Molony and another Australian Priest, George Gallen (who later taught me Canon Law at Manly from 1961—1964), were the official Australian Delegates to the Congress. As Molony notes, tongue-in-cheek, 'That I was not a layman apparently bothered no-one'. It was here that the core role of Laity in the Church became crystal-clear to him, and as he noted, 'Yet for lay people to undertake their own apostolate in the world they needed FORMATION . . . The only method of formation I could propose was that of the proven one called "See, Judge, Act" developed by Joseph Cardijn in Belgium'. Coming out of an era when *Catholic Action* had been defined as participation in the

---

4.   Perhaps inspiration for his 1976 book, *The Emergence of Political Catholicism in Italy*.

apostolate of the Hierarchy, Molony rejected the idea of Laity as 'Servants of the Sanctuary' as he termed it, seeing the Baptised as directly missioned to transform the world in the light of the Gospel. From this experience, and his reading of authors like Henri Godin (on the de-Christianisation of the Working Class) he records that he emerged with a determination to 'Plant the seeds of a Church fit and ready to change the world'.[5] It was a determination that he would carry home with him, as well as a methodology to fulfil it.

Influence Four: Immersion in the YCW Apostolate

In the long summer studies break of 1952, John Molony was in the UK, where 'The English Branch of the YCW had their headquarters in three broken-down old houses near the Oval in London'. Through the National Chaplain, Father Ted Mitchinson, and the several full-timers who lived and worked from those poor premises (where Molony notes, 'the food was terrible'), he came into contact with the working YCW in its local industrial contexts, and received with gratitude his first real exposure to the practical application of Cardijn's method. About this time, he writes, 'I concluded that the English model for the YCW was far and away the best form of Catholic Action'. At this time also, he attended a small international congress of YCW in Holland, seeing the YCW in its broader context. Returning from Holland by sea also gave birth to the signature hat affected by Molony from then on. It is a story you don't want to hear before lunch!

During his stay in the UK, John also met International YCW President Pat Keegan in London.[6] I am not sure what he felt about Keegan. His memoirs are very cautious on the topic. Later that same year, 1952, Molony worked for at least a full day with Keegan and Cardijn in Rome whence they had come to convince the Vatican of

---

5. Godin was a French YCW Chaplain. In 1943, with another priest, Yvan Daniel, he wrote a book *France: pays de mission?* In this work, he analysed the 'dechristianisation' of the working class in French cities and the need to develop new strategies.

6. Patrick Keegan was the first president of the IYCW from 1945 until the first International Council in 1957. He played a key role not only in the development of the English YCW but also the International YCW.

the innate worth of the YCW. I have no doubt that this was the final peg in the line of events that changed his life—meeting with the charismatic founder of the YCW (JOC) movement himself. I know others who trace the strength of their commitment back to that experience.[7] But whatever about that, John Molony was now a fully committed JOCIST himself.

There were doubtless other influences on his conversion. His exposure to the Worker Priest movement in Paris in 1952; his exposure to the political philosophy of Jacques Maritain; his meeting with Justin Simonds in 1953 when the Cardijn-influenced Melbourne Coadjutor was leading an Australian Pilgrimage to Europe; his meeting *en route* back to Australia with Vincent Giese of the legendary YCW Publishing House, Fides Press in Notre Dame Indiana. The concatenation of all these events brought him home with a passion for the apostolate that remains to this day, as evidenced by the list of his interests in a recent *curriculum vitae*. Cardijn's visit to Ballarat in 1958 would also have been an astounding boost, and so many more influences that we don't have time for this morning. I can only recommend that you take the time to read his autobiography. It will be time well spent.

I want to conclude with John's own words. It is a book I was given when I took up my first YCW Chaplaincy in the NSW city of Goulburn in 1967. It is one of four books I have carried with me over forty years. The others include St Thomas Aquinas' *Summa Theologica* (in Latin), Molony's *Roman Mould of the Australian Catholic Church*, and surprisingly, Robert Blair Kaiser's book, *Inside the Council*. About the book in question, Molony writes: 'My first book, and thus my major publication in those years was *Towards an Apostolic Laity* (Melbourne 1960). I had help with it from Vin Fennelly and Brian Burke. The book dealt exclusively with Catholic Action and in particular with the YCW. As a kind of guidebook for Priests, the contents are earnest, thoughtful, dry and certainly impersonal. I have often been surprised—stunned is perhaps a better word—when in later years, I have met Priests here and there who have thanked me for it. They said it was a great help to them in their priestly work in the Apostolate of Catholic Action'.

---

7. Including my wife, Judy (nee Crowe) who as a full-time extension worker in Southern NSW in the late sixties, met Cardijn and was inspired to continue in her work. It changed her life.

If John Neylon Molony came into this room today, I would line up to thank him for it (and many other things), even at the risk of stunning him once more. And I suspect I might not be on my own. My friends—John Neylon Molony, Pastor-formator, Historian and all-around Grace to this Nation.

Cardijn and Mondragon: YCW Origins of the Worker Co-operatives Complex

Race Mathews

Cardijn

Let me at the outset like earlier speakers pay tribute to the man to whose insights and example today's proceedings owe their inspiration and inception. Let me recall the response of Pope Pius XI when briefed by the young Josef Cardijn in the Vatican in 1924 on the progress and prospects of the then nascent Young Christian Workers Movement. As is well known, it reads:

> A last! Here is someone who talks to me about the masses, of saving the masses . . . A Church in which only the well-off are to be found is no longer Our Lord's Church. Our Lord founded the Church for the poor. That is why it is necessary to restore to him the working masses.[1]

Cardijn wrote in 1949 ''We have arrived at a decisive stage':

> The working-class must accept responsibility; it must share in the running of industry and industrial concerns . . . There is not other means of progress, either for the Church or for all humanity, if we do not accept this: that the working-class must have an equitable share in the administration of production; that the working-class should accept its responsibilities for production.[2]

---

1. De La Bedoyere, *The Cardijn Story*, 67.
2. Josef Cardijn, *The Hour of the Working Class* (Melbourne: YCW National Headquarters, 1949) 20, 12.

Action should be '*with* the working class, *by* the working class, *for* the working class', and the working class should be enabled to take greater control of their own affairs.[3] The prayer recited for many years at the opening of YCW meetings reads in part 'May our souls remain in Your Grace today, and may the soul of every worker who died on labour's battlefield rest in peace'.[4]

The emphasis throughout was on formation—on the inculcation of an informed Catholic conscience and consciousness. The conceptual framework—'Jocism', from *Jeunesse Ouvrière Chrétienne*—was formation through the organisation's 'Inquiry' or 'See, Judge and Act' approach, of enabling its members to apply moral principles within their workplaces and working lives. In modern conditions, Cardijn believed, 'the ordinary man did not find his primary source of identity and interest within the parish, but in his employment and his economic class'.[5]

A representative summary by an Australian YCW member and activist of the day, Leon Magree, reads:

> If you saw a problem you judged whether that problem will start again; you saw a situation, you judged whether that situation was right or wrong having regard to the principles you were trying to adhere to, in other words was there a conflict between what you saw happening in your workplace or community compared with what you thought the situation should be? Then having judged there was something wrong you took action. That action might have been as an individual or it might have been some group action'.[6]

---

3. De La Bedoyere , *Cardijn Story*, 31.
4. Val Noone, 'A New Youth for a New Australia': *Young Christian Workers Around 1960*, Paper for the Australian Association for the Study to Religions, Australian Catholic University, Aquinas Campus, Ballarat, 6–9 July 1995. 6.
5. Colin H Jory, *The Campion Society and Catholic Social Militancy in Australia 1929–1939* (Sydney: Harpham, 1986), 6.
6. Leon Magree. As interviewed by Richard Raxworthy for the Australian Credit Union Historical Society Co-operative, Melbourne, 3 November 1991. Tape 1 Side A of three Tapes. Transcript courtesy of the Australian Credit Union Archives, Sydney, 2007, 3.

Arizmendiarrieta

Working predominantly through the local Catholic Action and YCW groups, the Basque priest Don Jose Maria Arizmendiarrieta in his turn imparted new depth and duration to the formation process to impressive effect over an extended period from 1941 to 1956, in preparation for the inception of the great worker co-operatives complex at Mondragón. As recalled by a onetime protégé and co-founder of the co-operatives, José María Ormaechea:

> The Study Circles in *Acción Católica* and in JOC (Young Christian Workers Movement) continued at progressively higher levels . . . under the aegis of the Diocesan Secretariat in Vitoria, Father Arizmendi organized specialist courses on sociology to which he invited economics professors . . . His ecclesiastical training led him towards being a practical apostle. He not only tried to give guidelines on what should be the model for the ideal enterprise, but he put that social enterprise to which he aspired into practice.[7]

'In calculations we were making in 1956, we counted more than 2000 circles of study that he conducted. Some for religious and humanistic orientation; others for social orientation', Ormaechea wrote.[8] The report of an early study of the co-operatives by the Cornell University researchers William Foote Whyte and Kathleen King Whyte reads:

> Thus from 1941 on, Arizmendi conducted at least one study session every 2.7 days, not counting holidays and vacations, in addition to teaching his regular schedule. As one of his former students told us, 'He taught classes in religion and sociology— and really his religion classes were mainly sociology'. Sessions with those who had been his first students focused particularly on discussions of conflicts between labour and capital, reform of private enterprise management and the participation of workers in ownership . . . In his sermons and writings, he

7. José María Ormaechea,*The Mondragón Co-operative Experience* (Mondragón: The Mondragón Corporacion Cooperativa, 1991), 20. 'Arizmendi' as customarily abbreviated from 'Arizmendiarrieta'.
8. William Foote Whyte and Kathleen King Whyte, *Making Mondragón: The Growth and Dynamics of the Worker Co-operative Complex* (Ithaca NY: ILR Press, 1991), 32–33

stressed that work should not be seen as a punishment but as a means of self-realization. There should be dignity in any work. He stressed the need for co-operation and collective solidarity. He combined a social vision with an emphasis on education for technical knowledge and skills.[9]

A passage written a few days before his death in 1976 reads:

> Hand in hand, of one mind, renewed, united in work, through work, in our small land we shall create a more human environment for everyone and we shall improve this land. We shall include villages and towns in our new equality; the people and everything else: 'Ever forward'. Nobody shall be slave or master to anyone, everyone shall simply work for the benefit of everyone else, and we shall have to behave differently in the way we work. This shall be our human and progressive union—a union which can be created by the people.[10]

Imprisoned and narrowly escaping execution following service as a journalist with the Basque military in the Spanish Civil War, and refused permission by his bishop to study sociology at the University of Louvain in Belgium, Arizmendiarrieta was sent instead in 1941 to work under the more senior priests in the war-ravaged town of Mondragón, whose former arch-priest, Fr Joaquin Arin, had been one of seventeen Basque priests shot by Franco's victorious Nationalist forces. His pastoral duties were taken up during what was known as 'the hunger period':

> Working people were desperately poor and oppressed by unemployment, run-down and overcrowded housing, and an outbreak of tuberculosis. People spoke of the spirit of hopelessness. They saw themselves as a conquered people, living under a regime that offered neither political freedom nor economic opportunity.[11]

Embarking through the local Catholic Action and YCW organizations on a search for ways 'to guide people into action to solve the problems oppressing them', he initiated as his first step the creation

---

9. Whyte and Whyte, *Making Mondragón*, 29
10. Ormaechea, *The Mondragón Co-operative Experience*, 7.
11. Whyte and Whyte, *Making Mondragón*, 26.

of a medical clinic and a soccer club.[12] Following the rejection by the local steelworks of a request by him for admission to its apprenticeship school of boys who were unrelated to its employees, an independent technical school, the *Escuela Politécnica Profesional*, was formed, and opened in 1943 with twenty students. Adding a new level as soon as the students had completed the previous one, the school is seen by the authors of an early Cornell University study, William Foote Whyte and Kathleen King Whyte, as having 'provided the base for the creation and development of the co-operatives that would build the Mondragón complex'.[13]

Enabled at Arizmendiarrieta's initiative to proceed on the completion of the education available to them in Mondragón to study *in absentia* with the University of Zaragoza, eleven of the twenty young men enrolled by the *Escuela Politécnica Profesional* at its inception secured degrees in technical engineering from the university. In the early nineteen-fifties, five of them—Luis Usatorre, Jesus Larrañaga, Alfonso Gorroñogoitia, José María Ormaechea and Javier Ortubay—told Arizmendiarrieta that 'they were determined to start a new company organized along the lines they had been discussing'.[14]

What eventuated in 1956, as a handful of workers in a disused factory, using hand tools and sheet metal to make oil-fired heating and cooking stoves, is in 2013 a massive complex of some 260 manufacturing, retail, financial, agricultural, civil engineering and support cooperatives and associated entities, with jobs for 83,800 workers, and annual sales in excess of $US20 billion. The Basque region's largest industrial conglomerate and the fifth largest in Spain, the Mondragón co-operatives now own or joint venture some 114 local and overseas subsidiaries, and are committed to their conversion to employee ownership on a case-by-case basis, consistent with local laws, customs and other cultural and economic considerations.

As equal co-owners of their workplaces, members enjoy job security together with individual capital holdings, equal sharing of profits on a proportionate basis and an equal 'one member, one vote' say in their governance. Remuneration within the cooperatives is egalitarian, with the highest rates payable other than in exceptional circum-

---

12. Whyte and Whyte, *Making Mondragón*, 29.
13. Whyte and Whyte, *Making Mondragón*, 31.
14. Whyte and Whyte, *Making Mondragón*, 33.

stances being no greater than six and a half times the lowest. Members share at one remove in ownership of a unique system of secondary support co-operatives, from which the primary or frontline co-operatives draw resources including financial services, social insurance, education and training and research and development. Hybrid primary co-operatives within the group include its worker/consumer *Eroski* retail co-operative and worker/farmer agricultural co-operatives. Multi-stakeholder structuring plays a key role in endowing the co-operatives both individually and collectively with their impressive cohesiveness and resilience.

Reflective of the high priority attached by the primary co-operatives to the competitive advantage of cutting edge research and development is the augmenting of the original *Ikerlan* research and development support co-operative with thirteen sister bodies, specializing in the needs of particular aspects of manufacturing activity and product development. Annual outlays for research and development total some $75 million, and in 2010 21.4 per cent of sales comprised new products and services which had not existed five years earlier.

Faced as have been the co-operatives repeatedly throughout their existence by adverse trading circumstances, they have been able to avail themselves of significant flexibilities. For example, non-members employed on a temporary basis can be put off until conditions improve. Members can agree to forfeit or postpone entitlements such as one or more of their fourteen *per annum* pay packets or the payment of interest on their individual capital accounts, or in extreme circumstances authorize individual capital account draw-downs. Co-operatives experiencing reduced demand are able to transfer members to those where it is increasing, without detriment to their rights or entitlements. And supplementary capital can be accessed from centrally held inter-co-operative solidarity funds. Confronted in the aftermath of the Global Financial Crisis with circumstances, where unemployment was in excess nationally of twenty-five per cent, and among young people at around forty-five per cent, Mondragón was instrumental in helping hold keep jobless levels in the Basque region to under half the national average. 'Our commitment is not to capital but to the creation of sustainable jobs', Mondragón CEO Txema Gisasola states:

This is not magic. We are in this market, competing in the capitalist world, and the only difference is how we do things and why we do things. We have to be competitive, we have to be efficient, we have to have quality in our products and give satisfaction to our clients, and we have to be profitable. In that sense we are no different from anyone else. The difference is how we organize ourselves. Some will ask if [the co-operative structure] is a disadvantage, but it is the complete opposite. The company's workers are the owners of the project, so who is better than them to fight for its interests? They come to work because it is their project.[15]

Mondragón in America

No less are green shoots of Distributist initiative emerging from previously less hospitable soils. Announcing a formal partnership between his 850,000 member union and Mondragón in 2009, the United Steelworkers (USW) president Leo Gerard put its essence in the proverbial nutshell:

Too often we have seen Wall Street hollow out companies by draining their cash and assets and hollow out communities by shedding jobs and shutting plants. We need a new business model that invests in workers and invests in communities. We see Mondragón's co-operative model with 'one worker, one vote' ownership as a means to re-empower workers and make business accountable to Main Street instead of Wall Street[16]

'What we are announcing today represents a historic first, combining the world's largest industrial worker co-operative with one of the world's most progressive and forward-looking unions to work together so that our combined know-how and complementary visions can transform manufacturing practices in America', Mondragón Internacional president Josu Ugarte said.[17] A 2012 report by

---

15. Miles Johnson, 'Drivers of Change: Workers United', *Financial Times*, 21 March 2013.
16. Amy Dean, 'Why Unions are Going into the Co-op Business', *Yes! Magazine*, 5 March, 2013.
17. Erbin Crowell, 'Mondragón and the United Steelworkers: New Opportunity for the co-op and labor movements?', *Cooperative Grocer*, January-February 2010.

the USW in conjunction with Mondragón and the Ohio Employee Ownership Centre (OEOC) differentiates between union and traditional worker co-operatives on the basis of the capacity of workers in a union co-operative to appoint a management team, from within their own ranks or from outside the co-operative, to bargain collectively on issues including wages rates, health care and other benefit packages and a process for grievances and arbitration of workplace disputes. Mondragón's cooperative bank agreed in September 2013 to partner with the Washington based National Co-operative Bank in the creation of co-operative stakeholder businesses throughout the United States.[18]

Designedly modest, and consistent with both subsidiarity and Schumacher's great 'Small is beautiful' dictum, inspiration in the implementation of the USW/Mondragón collaboration has stemmed at the outset from examples such as of Cleveland's Evergreen Co-operatives, with thirty worker-owners currently cleaning an annual four million tons of local hospital laundry, and planning underway for the creation of a solar installers' co-operative and a greenhouse co-operative that grows high-end salad vegetables and herbs for the hospitals, universities and restaurants. The objective ultimately is the make 'Mondragón' a household word, and the adoption of its model an objective whose legitimacy is universally accepted, and to whose adoption communities and industries universally will aspire. Had Cardijn lived to witness the success of Mondragon its scope and character may well have surprised him, but it is unlikely that he would have been disappointed.

---

18. PRN Newswire 4 September 2013, accessed at http://finance.yahoo.com/news/laboral-kutxa-mondragon-bank-national-175900469.html

Cardijn's Trinomials: A vision and Method of Lay Apostolate Formation[1]

Stefan Gigacz

Introduction

By the time of Cardijn's death in 1967, the JOC existed in close to 100 countries around the world with millions of adherents.[2] And his *see, judge, act* method of formation for lay apostolate had been embedded in the documents of the recently completed Second Vatican Council.[3] Today, however, few people understand the philosophical roots of this concept which can be traced back to Aristotle and Thomas Aquinas.

Moreover, there was much more to the Cardijn approach than the see, judge, act, the very success of which has tended to overshadow other vital aspects of Cardijn's vision and method of lay apostolate formation. Often these other aspects were themselves expressed by Cardijn in the form of trinomial expressions, such as his 'by, with and for young workers' formula that evidently borrows from the "of the people, by the people, for the people' in Abraham Lincoln's famous Gettysburg Address.

---

1. An earlier and slightly different version of this paper was published in *Australian Catholic Youth Ministry, Theological and Pastoral Foundations of the Faithful Ministry*, edited by Christian Fini OMI and Christopher Ryan MGL (Melbourne: John Garratt, 2014).
2. In this paper I refer to the Young Christian Workers (YCW) movement by its French acronym, JOC, that is *Jeunesse Ouvrière Chrétienne*, except where referring specifically to the Australian or another English-speaking movement.
3. *Apostolicam Actuositatem* No 29; *Ad Gentes* No 21 (referring back to *Apostolicam Actuositatem*); *Gaudium et Spes*, where the method is applied in *Part II*; and *Dignitatis Humanae* No 8.

In this paper, I endeavour to revive the memory and explain the significance of several of these other Cardijn trinomials, particularly his 'three truths' of faith, experience and method, his baptismally-based conception of education, service and representation, and his ecclesiological trinomial of Church, laity and clergy.

Sources of the Cardijn Approach

To understand Cardijn and his success, it is essential to appreciate not only the context in which the JOC movement was born, but also the century of effort by various pioneers who laboured to enable the Church to reach out to the burgeoning working class that emerged from the industrial and democratic revolutions that swept nineteenth century Europe. It was a history of trial and error, mistakes and progress, often controversial, rarely conflict-free—a history that Cardijn drew upon consciously and carefully.

Although rarely cited directly, Cardijn's early writings are littered with references to the key players upon whose work he drew: the turbulent French priest Félicité de Lamennais and his colleagues, Frédéric Ozanam, founder of the Society of St Vincent de Paul; Alphonse Gratry, sometimes described as the greatest Catholic philosopher of the nineteenth century; Frédéric Le Play, a mining engineer turned sociologist and social reformer; Léon Ollé-Laprune, a great educator and philosopher inspired by Gratry, Ozanam and Le Play; Marc Sangnier's social action movement, *Le Sillon*; Catholic social reformers from Germany's industrial heartland; Christian socialist leaders of the British trade union movement; the Gospel-inspired mutualist, Pierre-Joseph Proudhon; and even Karl Marx himself.[4]

Against the backdrop of the French revolution and restoration, Lamennais was one of the first to systematically articulate a new vision for the Church epitomised in the motto of his newspaper, *L'Avenir*: 'God and freedom' and based not on a traditional church-state alliance but on a new Gospel-inspired alliance with the poor. It is remarkable and significant that Cardijn, seeking answers to the alienation from the Church of his own former schoolmates, should

---

4. Joseph Cardijn, *My reading*: <http://www.josephcardijn.com/reading> (Last accessed 18/06/2017)

turn at the age of fifteen to reading the works of Lamennais and his followers.

Although critical of Lamennais' split from the Church, young Frédéric Ozanam, who was close to several of his followers, remained convinced that it was possible to reconcile freedom and the Church. When a new wave of worker revolutions shook France and Europe in early 1848, Ozanam was one of a minority of Catholics who called upon the Church to side with the revolutionaries. Indeed, Ozanam perceived those events as a historic opportunity for the Church to change course. By the end of that year, however, the revolution had been defeated, leading to the installation of a restored French Empire. For Ozanam, it was the year that the Church 'lost the working class' as Pope Pius XI would later tell Cardijn.[5]

Nevertheless, the work of Lamennais, Ozanam and their generation was not in vain. Some forty years later, students led by Marc Sangnier at Stanislas University College in Paris began to promote study circles on social issues which soon developed into a movement which became known as *Le Sillon* (The Furrow) as their magazine was entitled. It was the Sillon which pioneered many of the educational methods that Cardijn would draw on in the development of the JOC. These methods in turn were adopted by other 'Specialised Catholic Action' movements that emerged and spread like wildfire across Europe from the late 1920s.

Emergence of the YCW and Specialised Catholic Action

Cardijn began work in 1912 as a curate in the parish of Our Lady at Laeken, a mixed suburb on the outskirts of Brussels, housing many industrial workers, domestic workers and others. Given responsibility for social work with women, within a year Cardijn developed a thousand-strong network of women activists, drawn mainly but not exclusively from the working class areas.

Working with Victoire Cappe, a self-described Christian feminist who had founded the *Syndicat de l'Aiguille* (Needle workers' Union) and others, Cardijn also launched a series of study circles for young female (teenage) workers. Soon after, he came into contact with Fernand Tonnet, a young bank worker, who had recently moved to

---

5. Henri Guillemin, *Histoire des catholiques français au XIXe siècle*, 249.

Laeken. Both Cappe and Tonnet were already familiar with the Sillon's educational techniques, as was Cardijn himself who had visited the Sillon in France in 1907. Indeed, the early groups of young teenage girl workers that Cardijn and Cappe formed were closely modelled on the work of the Sillon.[6]

World War I interrupted many of these efforts, with Cardijn imprisoned twice by the German occupiers. However, by 1919, the path was open for further development of study circles for young workers. Cardijn, Tonnet and others soon launched *La Jeunesse Syndicaliste* (Trade Union Youth) for young male workers, the embryo of the later JOC. Similar efforts were made with the female young workers. By 1922, the movement had begun to refine its trademark *see judge act* methodology, although that name was not yet in use. In 1924, the name *Jeunesse Ouvrière Chrétienne* (JOC), later translated as *Young Christian Workers* (YCW) was adopted.

Inevitably, tensions arose with other Catholic youth initiatives, particularly the *Belgian Association of Catholic Youth* (ACJB) which regarded the class-based orientation of the JOC as divisive. Moreover, Cardijn never hid the influence of the Sillon, which had been closed down in 1910 following a letter by Pius X to the French bishops, accusing the movement of 'escaping hierarchical control' and of being influenced by democratic and socialist tendencies.

In a dilemma, Cardinal Désiré Mercier found himself unable to approve the JOC. This left Cardijn with no option except to appeal directly to Pope Pius XI. In a storied meeting in March 1925, the pontiff of Catholic Action endorsed Cardijn's movement in a move later likened by Yves Congar to Innocent III's approval in 1210 of the religious order created by Francis of Assisi.[7] It was on this occasion that Pius XI, echoing Ozanam, uttered his statement, made famous by Cardijn, that 'the greatest scandal of the 19th century was the loss of the working class by the Church'.[8]

Pius XI's endorsement opened the way to the large-scale development of the movement. Across the border in France, the JOC

---

6. Stefan Gigacz, *The Sillon and the YCW, Towards an Understanding of the Origins of the YCW*, <http://www.sillon.net/the-sillon-and-the-ycw> (Last accessed 18/06/2017)

7. Stefan Gigacz, *Cardijn and Congar at Vatican II* (awaiting publication)

8. Joseph Cardijn, *A meeting with Pope Pius XI 1925*:< http://www.josephcardijn.com/meeting-with-pope-pius-xi > (Last accessed 18/06/2017)

methods were immediately recognised as those pioneered by the Sillon. Moreover, Cardijn had solved the problem of connecting a lay movement to the Church. As a priest and chaplain to the movement, Cardijn acted as intermediary between the hierarchical Church and the JOC, which like the Sillon, operated as an autonomous lay movement with its own democratically elected internal leadership. This was the real innovation of Cardijn's concept of Catholic Action, later known as 'Specialised Catholic Action', and which distinguished it from the hierarchically-controlled 'Italian' model.

Moreover, the success of the Cardijn model quickly led to its widespread adoption and 'specialisation' in other 'milieux' or social environments. Already by the late 1920s, similar movements emerged for high school students (Jeunesse Etudiante Chrétienne/Catholique or JEC in English Young Christian/Catholic Students or YCS), university students (JUC/TYCS), farm and rural workers (JAC), young people from business backgrounds (JIC), etc. By the mid 1930s, similarly constituted 'adult' movements targeting and organising workers, families, etc. had also developed.

By 1939 when the JOC began to be organised in Australia, it had spread to fifty countries, reaching its worldwide peak twenty-five years later during the early 1960s, precisely coinciding with the holding of the Second Vatican Council where Cardijn's concepts and methods would have such an impact.

The Cardijn Method

Although Cardijn has long been associated with the *see judge act* method, few people today know the origins of the method or indeed understand his own role in its development. Moreover, the 'Cardijn method' is often understood in a reductionist manner as if the *see judge act* comprises the whole while in reality, it is a complex combination of theory and practice with deep philosophical, theological, sociological and pedagogical roots.

However, with his gift for identifying the essentials, Cardijn managed to express much of this in a series of catchy trinomial expressions, including the *see judge act* and other aphorisms with which he has often become personally identified.

Here, I will endeavour to show how these phrases taken together form a profound educational praxis for socially transforming lay action in the world.

See Judge Act: Virtue Ethics as the Basis for Life-Centred Democratic Action

Cardijn's *see judge act* has often been often traced back to St Thomas Aquinas' analysis of the cardinal virtue of prudence:

> Prudence is "'right reason applied to action,'" as stated above (Article 2). Hence that which is the chief act of reason in regard to action must needs be the chief act of prudence. Now there are three such acts.
>
> The first is "'to take counsel,'" which belongs to discovery, for counsel is an act of inquiry, as stated above (I-II:14:1).
>
> The second act is "'to judge of what one has discovered,'" and this is an act of the speculative reason.
>
> But the practical reason, which is directed to action, goes further, and its third act is "'to command,'" which act consists in applying to action the things counselled and judged. And since this act approaches nearer to the end of the practical reason, it follows that it is the chief act of the practical reason, and consequently of prudence..[9]

The Vatican II Decree on the Lay Apostolate, *Apostolicam Actuosita-tem* confirms this linkage:

> Since formation for the apostolate cannot consist in merely theoretical instruction, from the beginning of their formation the laity should gradually and prudently learn how to view,

---

9. ST 2a2ae.47. The English is from Thomas Aquinas, Summa theologiae. Volume. 36: Prudence (2a2ae. 47–56). New Advent <http://www.newadvent.org/summa/3047.htm> (Last accessed 18/06/2017)

judge and do all things in the light of faith as well as to develop
and improve themselves along with others through doing.[10]

However, the development of the *see judge act* as a pedagogical
method also has broader historical roots linked to Le Play, Gratry,
Ollé-Laprune and the Sillon.

Frederic Le Play[11] was a French mining engineer who sought
to apply scientific methods to the search for solutions to the social
problems of industrialising Europe. His empirical 'method of social
observation' was adopted extensively in Catholic social action circles.
Cardijn himself was trained in this method at Louvain and many of
his early writings bear this imprint, such as his 500-question enquiry
into the situation of young workers in Belgium in 1922[12] and the two
editions of *Le Manuel de la JOC* (*The Manual of the YCW*) published
in 1925 and 1930.

Related to these efforts is the work of Alphonse Gratry,[13] whose
theory of inductive reasoning[14] was formulated in terms of sense,
intellect and will,[15] three faculties corresponding to the steps of the
see, judge, act. Or as Léon Ollé-Laprune later described it: reality,
reflection and resolution.[16]

A disciple of Le Play, Gratry and Ozanam, Ollé-Laprune[17] was a
committed lay apostle working within the French university system.
His most famous and influential work, *Le Prix de la Vie* (The price/

---

10. *Apostolicam Actuositatem*, No 29: < http://www.vatican.va/archive/hist_
    councils/ii_vatican_council/documents/vat-ii_decree_19651118_apostolicam-
    actuositatem_en.html> (Last accessed 18/06/2017) Cf Also *Compendium
    of the Social Doctrine of the Church* in No 547: *Acting with prudence*: <http://
    www.vatican.va/roman_curia/pontifical_councils/justpeace/documents/rc_
    pc_justpeace_doc_20060526_compendio-dott-soc_en.html> (Last accessed
    18/06/2017)

11. Pierre Guillaume Frédéric Le Play: < http://en.wikipedia.org/wiki/Le_Play >
    (Last accessed 18/06/2017)

12. Fiévez and Meert, *Joseph Cardijn*, Chapter 4, *Brussels*: <http://www.josephcardijn.
    com/chapter> (Last accessed 18/06/2017)

13. Alphonse Gratry: <http://www.gratry.net> (Last accessed 18/06/2017)

14. Julian Marias, *History of Philosophy*, at 309.

15. Julian Marias, *History of Philosophy*, at 309.

16. Léon Ollé-Laprune, *Eloge du Père Gratry*: <http://www.olle-laprune.net/eloge-
    du-pere-gratry> (Last accessed 18/06/2017) (My italics in the citation.)

17. Léon Ollé-Laprune: < http://www.olle-laprune.net > (Last accessed 18/06/2017)

prize of life) argued that 'everyone has something to achieve in life'.[18] Therefore, it was necessary to identify the right action to take. How to achieve this? Channelling Aristotle's analysis of the virtue of prudence, Ollé-Laprune gave the following answer:

> Everyone must apply themselves more than ever, better than ever, to courageously and faithfully consult the principles and the facts in order to become more than ever, better than ever able to see clearly, judge and decide, precisely because it is no longer fashionable to do so.[19]

And the reason that this was important was precisely because 'history appears to be democratising'. Hence, the need for 'a personal effort to raise up spirits and souls' capable of acting for the democratic good.

The Sillon's method of Democratic Education

Influenced by Ollé-Laprune, in 1892–93, Marc Sangnier and his fellow students at the Stanislas College in Paris launched a social issues study circle known as *The Crypt* after the basement in which they met.[20] In 1894, the group launched a magazine, *Le Sillon* (The Furrow) to promote their work. Gradually, they began to start new groups with a priority for targeting young factory workers.

Another Sillon leader, Jules Rimet, began to organise football competitions for these young workers. Formed by this experience, Rimet became a prominent football administrator eventually launching an international football competition with the apostolic aim of promoting peace and friendship between the former warring parties of World War I. We know this today as the FIFA World Cup.[21]

In 1899, Marc Sangnier described the Sillon method as follows:

---

18. Albert Bazaillas, *Une philosophie de la certitude de la vie – Léon Ollé-Laprune*: <https://fr.wikisource.org/wiki/Une_Philosophie_de_la_certitude_et_de_la_vie_-_L%C3%A9on_Oll%C3%A9-Laprune> (Last accessed 18/06/2017)

19. Léon Ollé-Laprune, *Le prix de la vie*, Préface à la 3ème édition: <http://www.olle-laprune.net/le-prix-de-la-vie---preface> (Last accessed 18/06/2017) (My italics in the citation.)

20. Marc Sangnier, *Le Crypte de Stanislas*: <http://www.sillon.net/la-crypte-de-stanislas> (Last accessed 18/06/2017)

21. Jules Rimet website: <http://www.julesrimet.org> (Last accessed 18/06/2017)

> Every citizen must know the state of the country; when the situation is bad, he must seek solutions; and lastly, having found the solutions, he must act.

By 1905, the study circles had become a 'movement', coining an influential definition of democracy as the form of 'social organisation that tends to maximise the conscience/consciousness and the responsibility of everyone.[22] Thus, the Sillon study circles explicitly transformed Le Play's method into a method of raising 'consciousness' of social issues[23] and linked it to the task of developing democratic "virtue."

Although the Sillon ended in 1910, its methods prospered. In 1921, Cardijn himself described his own work as enabling "the perfecting of this consciousness and responsibility of the most humble of popular citizens."[24] Similarly, in his 1944 Christmas Message on democracy, Pope Pius XII characterised a democratic regime as one in which each person is 'conscious of his own responsibility and of his own views'.[25]

The JOC and the See Judge Act

The emerging JOC movement explicitly drew on this heritage. A key 1922 document characterised the functioning of study circles for young workers as follows:

> First rule – Social initiation is based on the enquiry
> Second rule – The facts identified by the enquiry must be judged in the light of principles.
> Third rule – From ideas it is necessary to pass over to action.[26]

22. Marc Sangnier, *L'esprit démocratique*, 1905, 167. Note that in French the word 'conscience' corresponds to both conscience and consciousness in English.

23. Louis Cousin, *Vie et méthode du Sillon*, 1906, 98–99.

24. Joseph Cardijn, *Welcome to Marc Sangnier*, 1921:<http://www.josephcardijn.com/welcome-to-marc-sangnier> (Last accessed 18/06/2017)

25. Pope Pius XII, *Democracy and lasting peace, Christmas message 1944*: <https://www.papalencyclicals.net/Pius12/P12XMAS.HTML> (Last accessed 18/06/2017)

26. René Van Haudenard, *La formation sociale aux cercles d'études*, in *La Femme belge*, March 1922: <https://docs.google.com/document/d/1H2ID0t9_3SJgG5rh M9bsPA1bhlAI3YlY5mPVfdAe8WI/> (Last accessed 18/06/2017)

Fr René Van Haudenard explained it thus:

> A. Bad method. We propose to study the encyclical *Rerum Novarum*. The encyclical is divided into ten parts of which each part will take up one session; the explanation of the text will be made without commentary, or examples. Result: By the third meeting the members drift away; it is rare that it will not be necessary to soon abandon the program if one wishes to maintain the circle.

> B. Method advised. Detailed and successive enquiries on property, salary, work, etc. as they appear in the living environment (milieu).

> Each session will involve examining answers to a questionnaire. Quite naturally the doctrinal points raised in *Rerum Novarum* will be developed. Result: The members will take an interest in the matter under observation, a social sense will develop, understanding will deepen because people will recall the facts that were the point of departure.[27]

Soon after, a new expression began to emerge: 'see, judge, do', which by the late 1920s took definitive form: *see judge act*. In essence, this was the method that would catapult the JOC to the forefront of social action, particularly among young people, first in Belgium and France, and very soon after to other countries and continents.

What made the difference, it would seem, was the simple fact that Cardijn and his team had managed to encapsulate a then well-understood philosophy of social enquiry, prudential action and virtue-based democracy into three practical words that spelled out the method and could be easily learnt.

In ensuing years, the JOC expanded and refined the method into three stages that took on different names over time:

> a) Review of influence or review of life, or the personal enquiry, which involved applying the *see judge act* to facts and action from daily life each week.

---

27. René Van Haudenard, *La formation sociale aux cercles d'études* in *La Femme Belge*, March 1922: <https://docs.google.com/document/d/1H2ID0t9_3SJgG5rh M9bsPA1bhlAI3YlY5mPVfdAe8WI/> (Last accessed 18/06/2017)

b) Gospel meditation or Gospel enquiry, which involved using the *see judge act* to apply Jesus' example to the daily events of life.

c) Social enquiry, applying the *see judge act* to a particular topic, usually of current interest, and/or perhaps extending a personal or Gospel enquiry, such as the Australian road safety campaign.

Perhaps even more significantly, the JOC, beginning with Cardijn in Belgium in the late 1920s, developed an annual program incorporating the above elements, which was distributed widely through the *Bulletin des dirigeants* for young leaders and the *Notes de pastorale jociste* addressed to chaplains.

Divine Origin, Divine DMission and Divine Destiny: The Basis of Human Dignity

The Cardijn method also has deep theological foundations, which he again often expressed in the familiar pedagogical trinomial form .

Using some of his most eloquent and powerful language, he set out his conception of human dignity:

Young workers, are not machines, or animals or slaves. They are the sons, the collaborators, the heirs of God. 'He gave them power to become the sons of God... partakers of the Divine Nature.' That is their sole true destiny, the reason of their existence, their life, and their work, the source of all their rights and all their duties.

This destiny is not two-fold: on the one hand eternal, and on the other temporal, without any link or influence of one upon the other. There cannot be an eternal destiny by the side, at a distance from earthly life, unrelated to it.

The eternal destiny of each human being is incarnate, develops, and is achieved in temporal life always and everywhere-on earth as it is in heaven... The destiny of the little servant girl, the young apprentice, in their normal environment, the framework, the atmosphere of their life; in the midst of all their comrades, their closest neighbours, whom they must help conquer their temporal and eternal destiny.

This fundamental truth, which cannot be repeated too often, is the basis of the whole Y.C.W.[28]

As always— – and unlike Jacques Maritain, for example— – Cardijn here preferred to emphasise an Augustinian continuity between the temporal and eternal rather than a perhaps more scholastic dichotomy between the spiritual and temporal.

Simply put, young workers had a 'divine origin' ''and a 'divine destiny' that were united by their 'diving mission' or 'vocation.'[29]

Educate, Serve and Represent: A Baptismal Basis for Transformative Lay Action

For Cardijn, JOC action had three aims which he expressed in another of his triads as 'educating, serving and representing' young workers:

> Only an organisation of young workers with a view to the conquest of their eternal and temporal destiny can solve the essential and vital problem, which faces each and all young workers. An organisation for young workers, by young workers, between young workers.

> And for this, an organisation which is adapted and specialised to the age, conditions of life, the future, the eternal and temporal destiny of the young workers.

> An organisation which is local, regional and national, united, disciplined, autonomous, living, conquering, capable of influencing and leading the masses of the young workers in their daily life and their normal environment.

> An organisation which is at once and inseparably a school, a service, a representative body.[30]

---

28. Joseph Cardijn, *The three truths*: <http://www.josephcardijn.com/the-three-truths> (Last accessed 18/06/2017)

29. Joseph Cardijn, *Allocution*: <http://www.josephcardijn.com/allocution-of-canon-cardijn> (Last accessed 18/06/2017)

30. Joseph Cardijn, *The three truths*: <http://www.josephcardijn.com/the-three-truths> (Last accessed 18/06/2017)

Although Cardijn never says so in so many words, it is evident that this 'educate, serve, represent' is based on the classical formulation of Christ's mission as the prophet who educates, the priest who serves, and the king who represents or advocates for his people. In fact, it is highly likely that he borrowed this conception from the English Cardinal John Henry Newman, who wrote that "'Christ exercised His prophetical office in teaching',," in 'the priest's service when he died on the Cross', and in showing himself 'as a conqueror and a king, in rising from the dead . . . and in forming his Church to receive and rule' over the nations.[31]

Thus, for both Newman and Cardijn prophecy corresponded to education, and priesthood to service. On the other hand, for Newman, kingship corresponded to 'receiving and ruling' over the people whereas for Cardijn it corresponded to 'representation', giving a slightly different emphasis to the kingly office.

As the JOC in Belgium developed, this concept was reworked by the chaplains and theologians close to the movement including Paul Dabin SJ,[32] whose books on lay apostolate, Catholic Action and the royal priesthood of the faithful, later inspired Yves Congar in his classic *Lay People in the Church: A Study on the Theology of the Laity.*

In a key speech at Vatican II on *The royal priesthood of the laity,*[33] Belgian Bishop Emile-Joseph De Smedt, a close ally of Cardijn, introduced this concept, which is largely incorporated into Chapter II of *Lumen Gentium* on *The People of God.*[34] Significantly, the main drafter of *Lumen Gentium* was another longstanding collaborator of Cardijn, Mgr Gerard Philips, who had worked for many years as a chaplain to the YCS and promoting Specialised Catholic Action in Belgian seminaries.

---

31. John Henry Newman, *Sermon 5, The Three Offices of Christ*, in *Newman Reader*: <http://www.newmanreader.org/works/subjects/sermon5.html> (Accessed 25/05/2017)

32. Paul Dabin SJ, *Le sacerdoce royale des fidèles dans les livres saints* and *Le sacerdoce royale des fidèles dans la tradition ancienne.*

33. Bishop Emile-Joseph De Smedt, *The royal priesthood of the laity*: <https://docs.google.com/document/d/1ZkDKX9UwKw6xdRV_bdfFCiSav2a0xweSaSNcyk6CFBM/> (Last accessed 18/06/2017)

34. Vatican II, *Lumen Gentium*

Cardijn's Ecclesiology: The Irreplaceable, Specifically Lay Apostolate of Lay People

Cardijn's ecclesiological approach can also be discerned in another of his trinomials: Church, laity, priests.

First comes the mission of the Church as a whole:

> The mission of the Church, like the mission of Christ, is to restore the whole of humanity to God and to put the whole of creation back into the plan of divine love.

> The Church too must be the leaven of the world, the light of the world, the salt of the world. She must transform humanity, reveal the true way to all persons and make her grace available to them, so that the whole world may participate in the work of redemption through the complete collaboration to which it is called.

> But we must never forget that this is the mission of the entire Church: the whole Church must therefore be apostolic.[35]

The 'irreplaceable' role of lay people derives and follows from this mission of the whole Church:

> Lay people must receive the person, the life and the doctrine of Christ, so that, growing in grace and making Christ truly incarnate in their own life, they may carry this divine life not only within their own soul, but to all their brothers and sisters: at work, in their social capacity, in their environment, and in any institutions where they can exercise their influence or give witness to their Christianity.

> The people who are actually living and working in the ordinary circumstances of everyday life are the lay people, and it is up to them to carry out Christ's mission in all the different temporal sectors of life and to make the whole Church present there. I can never repeat this often enough: the lay apostolate is irreplaceable.

---

35. Joseph Cardijn, *Priests and laity in the Church's* mission: <http://www.josephcardijn.com/priests-and-laity> (Last accessed 18/06/2017)

And this also clarifies the role of the priest 'who must reveal God's plan to the faithful and make them aware of the place they occupy in it'.

> It is the priest's duty to bring each Christian to a discovery of his/her true mission, and, through teaching the Good News, to throw light on all those errors which beset laypeople on every side: false missions, false doctrines, false messiahs.

> The priest must reveal this message not only to those baptised, but to all people. He must be concerned particularly with those who are not baptised, and who are not yet part of the flock. The Church is for all humanity, belongs to everyone.

For Cardijn, the priest thus had a vital role in 'awakening' in lay people an understanding of their apostolate, and particularly in forming them for an 'authentic lay apostolate'. In this conception, lay people are "the frontline" of the Church, as Cardijn stated citing Pius XII, inverting the traditional hierarchically centred ecclesiology as well as anticipating Vatican II, situating the task of bishops and priests as in the service of lay people.

The Three Truths of Faith, Experience and Method

Cardijn synthesised much of the above in his memorable 1935 speech, *The three truths*:

> Three fundamental truths dominate and illuminate the problem of the working youth of the world. They inspire, explain, and direct us towards the solution that the YCW has to give:

> 1. A truth of faith. The eternal and temporal destiny of each young worker in particular and of all the young workers in general.

> 2. A truth of experience. The terrible contradiction which exists between the real state of the young workers and this eternal and temporal destiny.

> 3. A truth of pastoral practice or method. The necessity of a Catholic organisation of young workers with a view to the conquest of their eternal and temporal destiny.

What was the significance of this formulation? Cardijn's *see judge act* had been much criticised, indeed occasionally rejected, as somehow compromising the Gospel in a kind of situational ethic. Sometimes, this criticism was expressed in the form 'the Church evangelises in order to civilise, it does not civilise in order to evangelise'.[36]

The three truths are Cardijn's dialectical response to this critique, showing how the 'truth of faith' remains at the heart of the JOC message. Since it is 'contradicted' by the 'truth of experience' in the world, a method is required for transforming this reality, namely the JOC method of forming people capable of seeing, judging and acting through serving, educating and representing their communities.

This very debate re-emerged at Vatican II in the drafting of *Gaudium et Spes*. In its initial drafts, the schema took a traditional 'doctrinal' approach, starting from Church teaching. In November 1964, however, the conciliar commission responsible decided that the final versions should be drafted using the *see judge act* method.

The remarkable result is that the final version of *Gaudium et Spes*, compiled under the direction of Mgr Pierre Haubtmann, a French chaplain to the JOC and its adult counterpart, was formulated in terms of Cardijn's three truths with the *Introduction* setting out the reality of the world of our time; *Part I* with its Christ-centred anthropology presenting the Church's truth of faith; while *Part II* applies the *see judge act* method in the fields of family, social, economic, political life and world peace.

The See, Judge, Act and Religious Freedom

At Vatican II, Cardijn himself, having been created a cardinal by Pope Paul VI, also presented the *see judge act* as a method for educating people in the use of religious freedom:

---

36. Pope Pius XI in a letter to the French Social Week in 1936
    <http://www.icmica-miic.org/about-us/2013-06-04-16-36-42/europe/united-kingdom/249-themes/new-evangelization/167-the-radical-roots-of-the-new-evangelization.html> (Last accessed 18/06/2017)

> This interior freedom, even if it exists in germ as a natural gift in every human creature, requires a long education which can be summarised in three words: see, judge and act.

> I have never wanted young people to live in shelter from dangers, cut off from the milieu of their life and work.

> Rather I have shown confidence in their freedom in order to better educate that freedom. I helped them to see, judge and act by themselves... conscious of being responsible for their sisters and brothers in the whole world.

For Cardijn, then, the *see judge act*, as adopted by the Council, solved the Lamennais problem of "God and freedom." In the same vein, he also explicitly linked the *see judge act* to the Sillon project of maximising the consciousness and responsibility of each person as indeed *Dignitatis Humanae* does in its opening lines:

> A sense of the dignity of the human person has been impressing itself more and more deeply on the consciousness of contemporary man, and the demand is increasingly made that men should act on their own judgement, enjoying and making use of a responsible freedom.[37]

Thus, without ever using the word 'democracy', Vatican II in effect adopted the Sillon's method of democratic education as re-interpreted by Cardijn.

Cardijn and the new evangelisation

Among the bishops at Vatican II who fought for the adoption of the Cardijn method were men like Bishop Helder Camara, himself a pioneer JOC chaplain in Brazil, and co-founder of CELAM, the Latin American Catholic Bishops Conference. It was thus no surprise to find that CELAM adopted the *see judge act* method as the basis of its work at its groundbreaking 1968 conference in Medellin, Colombia. In turn, this led to its adoption as the method of choice for basic Christian/ecclesial communities that grew out of the Latin Ameri-

---

37. *Dignitatis humanae* §1.

can experience. Likewise, Gustavo Gutierrez, a former YCS chaplain, embodied it in the liberation theology movement that he inspired.[38]

Moreover, it was at Medellin that the expression 'new evangelisation' first emerged, clearly in reference to the adoption of the Cardijn method.[39] It was at the next CELAM conference in Puebla, Mexico in 1979 that Pope John Paul II adopted the expression and made it a cornerstone of his pontificate. Having met Cardijn in Belgium in 1947 as well as while studying in Rome, and having backed the phenomenological approach of *Gaudium et Spes*, there is no doubt that Wojtyla understood the linkage of the term 'new evangelisation' to the Cardijn method.

Elsewhere, Cardijn's methods were successfully appropriated by many other Catholic organisations, including the Vincentian tradition,[40] Franciscan missionaries,[41] Marist schools[42] and others. Similarly, it has become the basic method for many social justice oriented groups, including our own Australian Catholic Social Justice Council.[43]

The Brazilian educator, Paulo Freire, adopted the see judge act as the basis of his own method of 'conscientisation' through literacy education.[44] Later, Freire put his method to work in an ecumenical context with the World Council of Churches where he worked during the 1980s.

More recently, Pope Francis has once again given top billing to the Cardijn method with his environmental encyclical *Laudato Si'* adopting the see, judge, act as its basic framework.

---

38. Simon C Kim, *Theology of Context as the Theological Method of Virgilio Elizondo and Gustavo Gutiérrez*: <http://aladinrc.wrlc.org/bitstream/handle/1961/9728/Kim_cua_0043A_10224display.pdf?sequence=1> (Last accessed 18/06/2017)

39. Stefan Gigacz, *The radical roots of the new evangelisation*: <http://blogwatcherextra.blogspot.com/2014/09/cathblog-radical-roots-of-new.html> (Last accessed 18/06/2017)

40. See <The "'See, Judge, Act'" process (VinFormation)> (Last accessed 18/06/2017)

41. See <Comprehensive Course on Franciscan Missionary Charism, The See-Judge-Act Methodology> (Last accessed 18/06/2017)

42. See <Social justice a mode for action (Champagnat's Way)> (Last accessed 18/06/2017)

43. See <Reading the Signs of the Times (Australian Catholic Social Justice Commission > (Last accessed 18/06/2017)

44. Rich Gibson, *Paulo Freire and revolutionary pedagogy for social justice*: <http://richgibson.com/freirecriticaledu.htm> (Last accessed 18/06/2017) In fact, Gibson appears to believe that the see judge act originated with Freire.

A Vision of Lay Apostolate

Yet if there is one aspect of Cardijn's contribution to Vatican II that has fallen from view it is undoubtedly his conception of the specifically lay apostolate understood as the role of Christians transforming the world. Indeed, for Cardijn this role was a human as well as a Christian vocation, one that applied to those of other faiths or even none.

The forgetting of this lay apostolate is also certainly linked to the paradoxical decline of the Specialised Catholic Action movements whose task it was, and is, to promote such a vision. In this sense, Cardijn's work still remains to be rediscovered and reinterpreted for the future.

Just as Vatican II sought to take the Church back to its sources in the Scriptures and in the early Fathers of the Church, perhaps it is also time for the JOC and its sister movements to return to Cardijn and his own sources.Just as other great spiritualities of the Church, such as those of St Francis and St Ignatius, have continued to spawn new initiatives, so too perhaps the Cardijn spirituality and methodology will inspire not just a renewal of the original Cardijn movements, but also the development of new movements responding to the fresh challenges of the twenty-first century.

BIBLIOGRAPHY

Joseph Cardijn

Cardijn, Joseph, *Allocution*, 1935: <http://www.josephcardijn.com/allocution-of-canon-cardijn> (Last accessed 18/06/2017)

Cardijn, Joseph, *My reading*, 1955: <http://www.josephcardijn.com/reading> (Last accessed 18/06/2017) Cardijn, Joseph, *Priests and laity in the Church's mission*, 1951: <http://www.josephcardijn.com/priests-and-laity> (Last accessed 18/06/2017)

Cardijn, Joseph, *The three truths*, 1935: <http://www.josephcardijn.com/the-three-truths> (Last accessed 18/06/2017)

Cardijn, Joseph, *Welcome to Marc Sangnier*, 1921: <http://www.josephcardijn.com/welcome-to-marc-sangnier > (Last accessed 18/06/2017)

Church documents

Pontifical Council for Justice and Peace, *Compendium of the Social Doctrine of the Church*, Vatican City, Vatican, 2005.

Pope Pius XII, *Democracy and a lasting peace*, Christmas message 1944.

Vatican II, *Ad gentes, Decree on the missionary activity of the Church*, Vatican City: Vatican, 1965.

Vatican II, *Apostolicam Actuositatem, Decree on the Apostolate of the Laity*, Vatican City: Vatican, 1965.Vatican II, *Dignitatis humanae, Declaration on religious freedom*, Vatican City: Vatican, 1965.Vatican II, *Gaudium et Spes, Pastoral Constitution on the Church in the world of this time*, Vatican City: Vatican, 1965.Vatican II, *Lumen Gentium, Dogmatic Constitution on the Church*, Vatican City: Vatican, 1964.

Other references

Aquinas, Thomas, ST 2a2ae.47, *Summa theologiae, Vol. 36: Prudence* (2a2ae. 47–56). New Advent <http://www.newadvent.org/summa/3047.htm>

Albert Bazaillas, *Une philosophie de la certitude de la vie – Léon Ollé-Laprune*, Paris: Revue des Deux Mondes, 1899: <http://fr.wikisource.org/wiki/Une_Philosophie_de_la_certitude_et_de_la_vie_-_L%C3%A9on_Oll%C3%A9-Laprune> (Last accessed 18/06/2017)

Cousin, Louis, *Vie et doctrine du Sillon*, Paris: Sillon – Emmanuel Vitte, 1905

Paul Dabin SJ, *Le sacerdoce royale des fidèles dans les livres saints*, Paris – Gembloux: Bloud et Gay – Duculot, 1941.

Dabin, Paul SJ, *Le sacerdoce royale des fidèles dans la tradition ancienne*, Bruxelles – Paris: Desclée De Brouwer, 1950.

De Smedt, Bishop Emile-Joseph, *The royal priesthood of the laity*, Vatican II, 1963: <https://docs.google.com/document/d/1ZkDKX9UwKw6xdRV_bdfFCiSav2a0xweSaSNcyk6CFBM/edit> (Last accessed 18/06/2017)Fiévez, Marguerite and Meert, Jacques with the collaboration of Aubert, Roger, *Cardijn*, Preface by Don Helder Camara, Translated by Edward Mitchinson, London: YCW England, no date (1974).Gibson, Rich, *Paulo Freire and revolutionary pedagogy for social justice*, San Diego: San Diego State University, undated: <http://richgibson.com/freirecritica-ledu.htm> (Last accessed 18/06/2017)

Gigacz, Stefan, *Cardijn and Congar at Vatican II* (Awaiting publication)

Gigacz, Stefan, *The fractured memory of the lay movements*, 2004: <http://www.stefangigacz.com/healing-the-fractured-memory-of-the-lay-movements> (Last accessed 18/06/2017)

Gigacz, Stefan, *The radical roots of the new evangelisation*, 2012: CathNews Archives <http://cathnews.com/archives/cathblog-archive/14101-cathblog-the-radical-roots-of-the-new-evangeli-sation> (Last accessed 18/06/2017)

Gigacz, Stefan, *The Sillon and the YCW, Towards an understanding of the origins of the YCW* in Stefan Gigacz (Ed.), *First steps towards a history of the IYCW*, Brussels: International Cardijn Foundation, 2000: <http://www.sillon.net/the-sillon-and-the-ycw> (Last accessed 18/06/2017)

Guillemin, Henri, *Histoire des catholiques français au XIXe siècle (1815 – 1905)*, Genève – Paris – Montréal: Au milieu du monde, 1947.

Kim, Simon C., *Theology of Context as the Theological Method of Virgilio Elizondo and Gustavo Gutiérrez*, Washington DC, Catholic University of America, 2011: <http://hdl.handle.net/1961/9728> (Last accessed 18/06/2017)Marias, Julian, *History of Philosophy*, (Translated by Stanley Appelbaumand Clarence C. Strowbridge), New York: Courier Dover Publications, 1967Ollé-Laprune, Léon, *Eloge du Père Gratry*, Paris: Téqui – Lecoffre, 1896: <http://www.olle-laprune.net/eloge-du-pere-gratry> (Last accessed 18/06/2017)

Ollé-Laprune, Léon, *Le prix de la vie, Préface à la 3ème édition*, Paris, Bélin, 1896: <http://www.olle-laprune.net/le-prix-de-la-vie--preface> (Last accessed 18/06/2017)

Sangnier, Marc, *Le Crypte de Stanislas* in Marc Sangnier, *Autrefois*, Paris: Bloud et Gay, 1936: <http://www.sillon.net/la-crypte-de-stanislas> (Last accessed 18/06/2017)

Sangnier, Marc, *L'esprit démocratique*, Paris: Perrin, 1905.

Van Haudenard, René, *La formation sociale aux cercles d'études* in *La Femme Belge*, March 1922: <https://docs.google.com/document/d/1H2ID0t9_3SJgG5rhM9bsPA1bhlAI3YlY5mPVfdAe8WI/> (Last acccessed 18/06/2017)

Websites

http://www.josephcardijn.com (Last accessed 18/06/2017)
http://www.josephcardijn.fr (Last accessed 18/06/2017)
http://www.gratry.net (Last accessed 18/06/2017)
http://www.julesrimet.org (Last accessed 18/06/2017)
http://www.olle-laprune.net (Last accessed 18/06/2017)
http://www.sillon.net (Last accessed 18/06/2017)
http://www.ypduniversity.org (Last accessed 18/06/2017)

Wikipedia

Pierre Guillaume Frédéric Le Play: http://en.wikipedia.org/wiki/Le_
    Play (Last accessed 18/06/2017)

Remembering The YCW 1945–1965

Helen Praetz

Origins of the Research

This research started in 2009 from a conversation with Race Mathews about his research for his most recent doctorate.

He was aware of the need to record the memories of people while they were still alive and cogent. We agreed immediately that the research would be related to Race's work but would not be linked in directly. So we drew up a bit of a list of possible people and I started to formulate the research questions with a view to getting a research grant.

Having a research grant from Catholic Theological College was important as it gave institutional cover when recruiting informants. I could tell informants that what they said was going on the record and the oral archive would be housed in the Melbourne College of Divinity Research Repository.

I was interested in recording the voices of those who remembered the heyday of Catholic Action in Australia, which was expressed in a whole range of organisations, including the YCW, but also the Campion Society, the Catholic Worker, the National Catholic Rural Movement, the Newman Society and others. I wanted those I interviewed to describe the sources of their own, or their parents' ideas, the organisations they were part of, including their activities, formation and education, and the legacies of that period for the Church and for the society. I interviewed eleven people between March 2009 and November 2010.

Memories of the YCW

While many of those interviewed mentioned the YCW, four of them strongly focused on it. Two spoke of their own involvement, namely Kevin Peoples and Jim Ross. The accounts that they gave show something of the extraordinary influence that the YCW had on their subsequent lives and activities. We are fortunate indeed that Kevin Peoples has published his memoir which makes palpable the excitement and special nature of formation that he received through the gospel discussions and especially through the enquiry method which shaped his thinking over his lifetime. As he said, it was heady stuff.

Jim Ross describes the key part that he played in developing and expanding the reach of the YCW in the 1950s. As a paid organiser, he operated at the highest levels of the YCW and shaped the methods and processes that he describes in educating young workers, in *conscientising* them, in the tradition of Paulo Friere. He outlines the initial 12 week training program for new groups which introduced them to the YCW and set out the framework. Meetings were based on a gospel reflection, a census when they identified other young people and tried to make contact with them; items of interest which was an attempt to continue to explore the reality of their lives and what was happening; and facts of action, where people had taken action and the group reflected on that.

Jim Ross sees the enquiry method as a process undertaken every week which became automatic over time. He describes it as a formalised campaign based around themes – to look at the situation in their daily lives; to reflect on that in the light of Christian social principles and then to decide how to address the contradiction between that reality and experience and those principles. I understand that he is preparing a memoir which will add greatly to our understanding and to the literature in this area.

Both interviews spoke of the importance of the priests' influence in the work of the YCW. The other two people in my research discussed the YCW from their perspectives as priests.

Fr Cyril Hally recalled the importance of Fr Charlie Mayne SJ, and visiting YCW leaders, including Ted Long, Fr Lombard and Fr Charlie McCann, in his own seminary formation. He supported the YCW because he judged that the development of young men in two years in the YCW was more effective than the formation of seminarians in seven years. He describes his contacts with the international leadership of the YCW and the significance of it as a lay movement in a clerical church.

John Molony recalled his life as a priest and his involvement with the YCW as a young curate in Ballarat. Again, he dwelt on the importance of the lay leadership and the stifling effects of clericism. His several volumes of memoirs amplify these views.

The above interviews give some substance to the question of why the YCW flourished, though they are all very serious accounts. There is little mention of the importance of the football competition, the social life including the dances which were happy dating grounds, and that the meetings and other activities offered escape from parental supervision.

Why Did the YCW Die Away?

All these informants speak of Church factors: the changes that the Second Vatican Council brought to Church and how the parish became central to the work of the pilgrim church, thereby downgrading special ministries. As Jim Ross noted, it had a strange impact because while the Council endorsed the things that the YCW and other groups had been saying for 20 years, the Catholic Action movements all died away rapidly thereafter. Not mentioned but important is the fact the many of the inspiring young priests left the priesthood and no longer assisted the development of YCW groups.

What I would like to see is some research which examines economic and social factors in the decline of the YCW and the loss to the Church that is entailed.

Members of the YCW were young, very, and changes in the labour market and education affected this group. While full-time employment of young people in entry level jobs had been declining since the Second World War in Australia, by 1970, structural changes in the labour market and the elimination largely of entry level jobs meant that the nature and number of young workers had changed significantly. After near full employment during the post-war years, youth unemployment preoccupied policy makers and was a major election issue from the early 1970s when the unemployment rate for fifteen to nineteen year olds was twenty-five per cent.

During the immediate post-war period, most young people left school at Year 10 to go to full-time work, including apprenticeship.

Increasingly, though, young people combined working part-time and schooling; by 1981, one fifth of young people were in that category.

Participation in education became a policy goal during the same period. During the immediate post-war period, most young people left school at Year 10 aged about fifteen and entered full-time work: by the 1970s, most sixteen year-olds were at school and completing Year 11. In 1970, the upper secondary curriculum was directed to the small proportion of young people who continued straight on to University but greater diversity of curriculum and alternative credentials were becoming established. By 1983, the policy goal was to make schools and TAFE attractive to the great proportion of ifteen to nineteen year olds. Extended education rather than early entry to work was preferred.

The extended dependency of young people, their primary identification as students rather than as workers and their instrumental attachment to the labour market via part-time work all point to the drying up of the market that was tapped by the YCW. Why the YCS did not step into this space is a matter of potential research.

Successful Interviewing

I applaud the intention of the organisers to record the testimonies of those who are keepers of the memory of these days. The informants that I had the pleasure of meeting were willing and many were enthusiastic participants in the recording of their stories. I found the following to be helpful.

1. Clearly establish the time, place and expectations of the interview. Arrive on time with reliable, familiar recording equipment.
2. Before you go, become as fully informed as you can be about the person you are interviewing .
3. Re-iterate the purpose of the interview and reconfirm permission for this interview to form part of the research project.
4. Open the interview by identifying the person, place and date and move to a general question which opens up the terrain, for example, 'What can you tell me about your early days in the YCW?'
5. Have a schedule of questions to ensure the major points are covered but listen attentively for any new leads to follow up and do so.

6. Allow the interviewee to reflect and think out answers and let them find the word rather than prompt.
7. Keep your opinions to yourself. Your job is to get the interviewee to open up to you not the reverse.
8. Accept that the interviewee's definition of reality and the historical record might differ. This is a record of what the interviewee can remember.
9. Thank the interviewee with a letter in the following week.
10. Send a copy of the interview and the transcript, if any, to the interviewee for any corrections, emendations or elaborations.

The interviews can be found in Helen Praetz (ed) 'The Church in Springtime: Remembering Catholic Action 1940-1965' (2011): <http://repository.divinity.edu.au/896/1/Matthews,_Race_-_The_Church_in_Springtime.PDF>

Cardijn Studies 1/2017

'The Sacred Worked In The Factory':
Joseph Cardijn and BA (Bob) Santamaria, Two Modes of Catholic Social Action, Mid -Twentieth Century. A Comparison

Kevin Peoples

'One of the difficult things is not to change society – but to change yourself.'

Nelson Mandela

Santamaria

Santamaria and Jocism were not a good fit.

Consequently, early in 1944, Santamaria engaged in argument with Archbishop Justin Simonds, Coadjutor Bishop of Melbourne. Simonds was the Episcopal Chair of the Young Christian Workers Movement. He understood the Jocist system well. He was to become increasingly sceptical of Santamaria's version of Catholic Action.

Santamaria was the Deputy Director of the Australian National Secretariat of Catholic Action. In 1944 he was twenty-eight years of age.

Santamaria found the Jocist model too limiting for the social and political action he had in mind for adults.

He told Simonds that the Jocist model of Catholic Action, as practised by the YCW, was essentially a parish affair, limited to the direct religious apostolate. Its task was to encourage young workers to practise their faith: attend mass, receive the sacraments, avoid temptation and marry within the Church.

The YCW, he argued, had no social or political apostolate.

Cardijn

Cardijn developed the Jocist model of Catholic Action.

His working class family was uneducated and poor but enterprising. Cardijn arrived as a curate at Laeken, Brussels suffering from the effects of pleurisy. His parish priest welcomed him as an invalid and commented 'My parish organizations are sunk'.

Within one year Cardijn knew every young worker in the parish. Not just their names and addresses, but where they worked and what were their worker problems. He met them outside the factory gates as they left work. He was an extraordinary communicator. Cardijn was a salesman but not your typical religious salesman. He knew that many of his young workers had deserted their childhood faith.

Cardijn was different. Unlike the clergy in general:

- he did not try to sell the young workers abstract notions of a God in heaven;
- he did not try to sell them the eternal truths of Catholicism;
- he did not ask them to repent or to attend Mass;
- nor was he political in any ideological sense;
- he did not try to replace capitalism with socialism or with any new society based on the Church's social teaching;
- he was more interested in people than ideas.

So what was he doing? He had one big idea which burnt within him.

The big idea that drove him was this: the contradiction between the dignity of each young worker as a child of God and the corruption of that idea through their demeaning labouring conditions.

Cardijn wanted to solve the worker problem.

This model of Catholic social action was more interested in justice than any radical political change. It was a practical model, seeking incremental change and operating at a local level.

But of course it was more than this.

In a sense he was not operating at a political level at all. Political change may occur, must occur, but the drivers of change were spiritual and so was the outcome. The outcome Cardijn sought was a working environment shot through with the loving spirit of Christ.

Cardijn rejected the notion that religion was somehow separate from life. To understand Cardijn and Jocism you have to understand his attempt to integrate the two—religion and life, the sacred and the secular.

Cardijn's model of social action was based on one apparently simple idea.

He believed that each young worker had been called by God to live out their sacred and irreplaceable vocation and mission in the world. Their mission was to improve the conditions of all young workers.

Cardijn's apparently simple idea captured youth around the world. In its universality, the mission resembled Marxism. Each young worker, whatever their religion, whatever their race, gender or colour, whatever their culture or education, had a God-given value and an individual mission.

Cardijn's foundational idea was profound and went far deeper than whether young workers met their Easter dues or attended Mass or spoke with a foul tongue.

Cardijn had made his first step in injecting the sacred into the secular. The sacred worked in the factory.

Cardijn began his model of social action modestly. He began with the worker problem – not his problem, but the problems experienced by young workers. He looked to individuals to act.

His immediate problem was how to make young workers aware of their special dignity, their unique mission and their responsibility to their fellow workers. It was one thing to tell them. It was another to get them to live it. It would take time.

Santamaria

How did Santamaria begin?

He was a brilliant student at school and university. He won scholarships. Like Cardijn he came from humble beginnings. Santamaria's ancestors were Italian peasants and fishermen.

As with Cardijn, Santamaria loved his church. He made a name for himself as a debater at the University of Melbourne. He was an orator at a very young age. He had a great gift of thinking quickly on his feet. Of involving his audience with his passion.

He enjoyed centre stage. In 1937, he brought a majority of the audience at the University of Melbourne to their feet as they joined him in the ringing cry of 'Long Live Christ the King' at the end of a debate on the Spanish Civil War.

He wanted to work for the Church. He joined the Campion Society, a group of older Catholic intellectuals with connections to Melbourne University.

He was more interested in ideas than people.

He was an impatient young man, restless, bursting with energy. He could see what had to be done and couldn't understand why the older Campions didn't act.

He wanted them to start a newspaper. They hesitated. Without consulting he approached Archbishop Mannix and gained permission. So began the 'Catholic Worker'. He wrote virtually all the first edition himself and sent a copy to Hilaire Belloc, Joseph Stalin and Pope Pius X1.

Santamaria's main idea appeared in bold print: 'It's a fight. But we have been fighting for two thousand years. Victory has always been ours. It will be ours again, for our leader is Christ the King, our standard is the Cross'.

The young Bob was at war with society. He saw the world as a battlefield. The Church was under threat. Everywhere he looked he saw a persecuted Church. He, as with his Church, was engaged in a battle between good and evil. This was fortress Catholicism.

Bob was a journalist—a propagandist. A man of rhetoric. An instinctive politician. He understood the importance of ideas. He appealed to minds. He cast his net wide. He was interested in power and influence.

Think of Cardijn here. Already there are significant differences.

Cardijn operated at a much smaller scale. Bob's first impulse was to start a newspaper. All his adult life he had a newspaper. At forty-eight he had his own TV program. At sevety-three he began a new journal—*AD 2000*.

He was sure of himself, sure of his beliefs. He belonged to the One True Church. He understood his religion as a rational set of beliefs.

He was thrilled with the two papal encyclicals, *Rerum Novarum* (1891) and *Quadragesimo Anno* (1931). He thought the Church's social teachings had the answers to the world's problems.

Catholics needed to become militant. To engage in a political struggle. A dangerous strategy in a pluralist and secular society with a history of sectarianism.

He thought Australian society was essentially pagan. He was no friend of the 18th centuries Enlightenment philosophers whose values helped make the French Revolution; a revolution which placed an exaggerated emphasis on individual freedoms and human rights, liberalism and democracy.

He felt alienated from the industrial revolution with its urbanization, factories, slums, unions and left-wing politics.

If he could, he would turn it all back. The Church had to fight back, to engage the enemy. The enemy that had displaced his Church from the centre of power; that had deprived the pope of the papal states; that had separated the church from the state.

Cardijn

Cardijn was nine when *Rerum Novarum* was published. Like Bob he too was thrilled. Through his studies he learnt that the pope was sympathetic to the workers. The pope had endorsed the right of working men to form unions. The pope had recognized the problems that workers faced in the factories.

Cardijn read the encyclical to his father who could not read.

Santamaria

Santamaria was critical of Capitalism. He, like the Campions, thought that the Great Depression (1929–1932) had virtually destroyed Capitalism.

Like the Campions he saw an opportunity for the Church's social teaching. His interest was in implementing policy. His aim was radical. The scope of his task breathtaking.

He wanted to Christianise Australia. Not in a direct proselytizing sense but rather to establish in Australia a new economic, political and social order conducive to religion

When he said Christian he meant Catholic.

The Catholic weekly newspaper in Melbourne, *The Advocate* was critical of the first edition of the 'Catholic Worker'. Far too radical. Santamaria set out to defeat paganism, liberalism and secularism and destroy what was left of capitalism.

And he would begin with the National Catholic Rural Movement. The Rural Movement would create a great agrarian civilization based on the Church's teachings.

Cardijn

Cardijn started his movement with a small group of leaders whom he trained. He then formed other small groups, separate girls and boys, and he developed his mode of action. Eventually he developed his See, Judge and Act model or the Enquiry method.

Through the enquiry method, the movement would progress, young workers would learn through action and reflection, conditions in factories would improve.

He would not do the enquiry. The church would not do the enquiry. The intellectuals would not do the enquiry. The young workers would do the enquiry. They would see what the situation was in their workplace. When they had the facts, they would cast a judgment on those facts. Their measuring stick would be the Jesus of the gospels: 'Whatever you do to the least of my breathen you do unto me.'

The inquiry method would lead young workers to experience the contradiction between the real and the ideal. He called this experience a formation in life.

His inquiry method grounded action in this world. This method was his second injection of the sacred into the secular.

This was a movement that worked from the bottom up.

Santamaria

How did the young Santamaria go about setting up his movement? He studied the problems facing the farming community in Australia. He read all he could and he wrote a report. He described the problems and he provided the solutions.

He did all this from his office in Collins Street. He never consulted one farmer. This was a movement that worked from the top down.

He came up with a set of policies. These were to be implemented by his members. The most important policy was the 'independent farm'. Farmers must become self sufficient. Farmers should diversify and ditch the specialized or one-crop model of farming. Cooperatives and credit unions would replace the usurious banks.

It all looked political. It was easy to miss the religion?

It was there but not in a personal sense. Santamaria told his members that farming was a special calling, not a commercial exercise.

Farmers were close to God – God's people. It was natural to man. Natural to the family. Man had always tilled the soil. It was God's way.

Urbanization and religion were incompatible. Farmers had independence; they owned their own property; they could think for themselves. They would stand against all forms of totalitarianism. They would not come under the influence of trade union leaders, communists and socialists.

He told them they had a mission and their mission was religious. Catholicism would flourish. He told them rural Catholics practised their religion at rates higher than their urban cousins. He had the statistics. Families would flourish. Farmers had more children than people in cities. More statistics. It was heady stuff.

His program was political. Bob wanted to open up the land. He wanted governments to provide water where there was no water. Regional towns where there were none. The regions needed schools and universities, libraries and cultural activities to make the towns attractive and keep families in the country. He deplored the state of many homes in rural Australia. He wanted the same access to domestic amenities in the home that families in cities had.

He urged his members to ignore private banks which encumbered farmers in debt. He urged them to ignore overseas markets and concentrate on local markets. He recommended a modest income for God's people.

Like Cardijn he set up small groups based on the parish, each with a chaplain. Few chaplains understood Catholic Action. Fewer still understood the Rural Movement.

Nevertheless, there was an extraordinary urgency about the whole enterprise. Santamaria wanted groups formed throughout Australia. The rural bishops supported him.

Santamaria was more interested in the task than the formation of his members. Formation was a distraction. If he thought about it at all he saw it as knowledge. Formation in life he never understood.

His movement spread like wildfire across the nation. Structures were put in place. Chaplains were recruited. Pamphlets were published. Articles were written. Diagrams drawn, hierarchies established. A weekly newspaper, 'Rural Life' was sent to each member. He expected his members to see the urgency of his vision and implement his policies.

After an initial interest in Cardijn's enquiry method Santamaria dropped it. Too slow. Suitable for young people but not adults. Too much freedom to individuals. What was required was a highly disciplined and coordinated body of men. A single-force. Individual action was ineffective. He wanted the 'best men'; the born leaders. He rarely acknowledged rural movement women. His habit of acting was authoritarian.

After one year in operation, he was telling those Rural Movement members who failed to act to move out and make room for those who would. He bemoaned to his friends that the wrong people were being recruited. Too few were apostolic.

He felt hamstrung by the limitations of Catholic Action which forbade party political action. He wanted his members to permeate rural organizations. In 1948 he gave this idea a religious ring—the apostolate of institutions. The members owed their allegiance to him and the Rural Movement—not to the community organization they joined.

Catholics were infiltrating society. In its method of acting, the Rural Movement resembled the Communist Party. When I joined it in 1959 it was well dead.

I'll conclude here. There is enough above for you to get a sense of the two men and how their ideas differed. Cardijn died, a Cardinal, in 1967. Santamaria remained a warrior to the end—1998. His last fight was to restore the old church, destroyed in part by the Second Vatican Council and the cultural impulses of the 1960s.

The YCW, Community Empowerment, And The Establishment Of The Community Legal Centre Movement

John Finlayson

Stefan asked me to talk about the Fitzroy Legal Service and the early history of community legal centres. I think I should start with Cardijn because he inspired me and the YCW inspired me. In fact the YCW changed my life and created opportunities for me to take responsibility in social action. Without the YCW I don't know what I would be but I would be a pretty lost soul I think.

My background leading into the YCW was that I worked in a foundry. I worked there for about six years and it was during this time that I started to address some of the industrial rights that young apprentices in this workplace had. I was one of those apprentices. I would keep coming back to my weekly meeting at Highett YCW to address methodology—the see judge act method which I really understood. And it inspired me through friendship with young people in my workplace that I could go back to a base and I could reflect on that and I could plan my action for the next day or next week inside that workplace. In particular some of the occupational health and safety issues in foundries.

Foundries were very dirty places and things were happening in the foundry industry. I'm talking the 1960s—the first half of the 1960s particularly. I ended up in a situation where I got involved so heavily with the rights of the young workers that we began to challenge the company and how they dealt with workers generally. I got into a lot of trouble actually because I suggested to the managing director that probably the most effective way to cause development and improve the company was to give the opportunity to all workers to become part owners of the factory as well. He suggested I was going down the communist line and wanted to know who was influencing me. I said the YCW and he said 'that's Catholic isn't it?' I said 'yes'. He said he was

Catholic, and I said that he should know about them then. He told me that was really dangerous and gave me notice that if he saw me trying to influence or communicate with another young worker in that workplace then that was out the door. So that was the end of my proposal to try and unite the workers in part ownership of the company.

Around about that same time I met Cardinal Cardijn. I did not know I was going to meet him but a bloke called Frank Hornby who was mentioned before, a fantastic guy, asked me to come along and I was going to go along to meet this important bloke. He picked me up in his motor car because I didn't have a car at that time and took me over to Caulfield to the Chaplain's residence. Paul Willy was there and Kevin Smith was there and Cardijn was there, this fellow who I had heard so much about and he wanted to talk to me and no one else. And what he wanted to talk to me about was what I was doing in my workplace. He asked me a lot of questions about each one of those young people who were apprentices and what were the conditions of the workplaces and what were my strategies and methodology and what was my thinking. He was the first person in my life who said, 'you've got those apprentices there but there are three apprentices in that pattern shop down the way, do you get to see them?' I said 'no' and he said: 'Well start to make opportunities so you can and start talking to them about the things you're talking about with those apprentices in the foundry part'. And that was the first time I saw this guy trying to get me to see beyond my own situation to the wider picture.

There was a comment about Cardijn thinking small, but this guy had a massive vision and it inspired me and within six months I ended up becoming a full time worker with the YCW for the next four years.

After I left the YCW I went back into a workplace and started doing the same things I had been doing as an apprentice. I went back into a foundry in Moorabbin where there were about three or four young people, and I also started focusing on some of the adults because I thought there was a lot of injustice in that workplace. I lasted there for about thirteen months or so and I was asked to leave because of the influence I was having. They told me they did not want communists in the workplace. So they retrenched me.

Then I got involved as a community youth worker in the Fitzroy Community Youth Centre. And during the early part of that period I was involved with a footy team that had been a YCW footy team organised by the local priest. So I took on that role as well as the youth worker role, but it was through my involvement with the footy team that I discovered lots of these young people getting in trouble with the police and the legal system, and also that there were no legal services. I discovered the Legal Aid Committee that existed at that time but you had to give them four months notice about legal representation and of course all the young people being charged were going to the children's court or magistrate's court well inside four months so none of them were eligible. So after referring fourteen—I helped fill out the forms with them—none of them got represented and I got very frustrated with that and I thought we ought to create something of our own.

During this same period I started setting up some young people's groups across Fitzroy, Collingwood and Carlton using the same YCW method. You can still do it without having to be Catholic—with your reflection having to be Catholic—but it is the method that I used and I found that method really worked because when you begin to inspire young people they become decision makers of their own day-to-day activates outside of and in workplaces. They loved to take responsibility. I would say that even today. The way to reach young people is to give them the opportunity to take responsibility. That is empowerment and I believe in empowerment very strongly.

So with that approach we decided to try to create our own legal service. I was really hell-bent on wanting to do it but I did nott know much about lawyers and the law. But I knew two blokes who were involved in the law, one was an articled clerk and the other was a law student; one was Lou Hill and the other was Mick O'Brien. Their role was to get hold of some lawyers. My job was to get young people to a public meeting and get hold of Council who were my bosses anyway. Over a six-month period this happened and like Cardijn you don't rush in, you get your networks set up.[1]

---

1. O'Brien and Hill, who, together with Finlayson: '. . . organised the December 1972 public meeting which led to the creation of the Fitzroy Legal Service . . . had all been involved in some capacity with the Young Christian Workers' (John Chesterman, 'Law and the New Left: a History of the Fitzroy Legal Service 1972–1994', PhD, Melbourne University, 1994, 55–58). O'Brien chaired the meeting. Also, Finlayson cites the influence of Paulo Freire's *Pedagogy of the Oppressed* to his initiation of the FLS (Chesterman, 64–5); Stefan Gigacz in turn provides evidence that the YCW contributed to Freire's famous praxis and 'conscientisation' methods: <http://cardijnresearch.blogspot.com.au/2012/08/paolo-freire-ycw-and-cardijn.html>

At the same time I was involved in another movement, the Draft Resistance Movement, which played an important role for me and lots of other young people who were dissatisfied with the government over national conscription. I knew people who didn't fill out their draft papers went to jail for two years, which was totally unjust. The authorities always seemed to target people who didn't have the right to vote. At that stage you did not have the right to vote in general elections until you turned twenty-one years of age. People conscripted into the army were twenty year olds who did not have the right to vote, yet were treated like factory fodder to go to one place, the Vietnam war, which I was totally opposed to. I had relationships through the YCW with Vietnamese young fellows and they were beautiful people so why were we trying to blow these dudes away, whose war was it? So lots of us were part of this movement; some young people refused to fill out their draft papers and were anti conscription. Some were working underground, those who refused to fill out their draft papers took the risk—they knew that if arrested they would be serving two years jail unless they could show they were conscientious objectors. Most of these young people weren't conscientious objectors they were opponents of the draft itself and it was very political. As far as I am concerned YCW is political and always has been ever since I've joined it and have known from the age of sixteen. The political is the justice, the political is the empowerment and the decision-making and we can do this.

So I was asked to help organise a public gathering and at the time I was the caretaker of Lowana,[2] don't know if you remember that place? A number of organisations had approached me. Organisations such as the DMZ Bookshop which was a young peoples draft resistence action group connected with the social left of the ALP and also those groups connected to Harry van Moorst—do not know if you know him.[3] They were great leaders of demonstrations and anti war action against the Vietnam war. I said yes they could have a fundraising function at Lowana, it's a good place because at that time there's no training going on over the next two months. So we held this function there.

---

2. The villa 'Lowana' was the YCW Girls training centre at Brighton.
3. Harry van Moorst was a high-profile anti-war activist in the 1960s and 70s, and the vice-chairperson of the Vietnam Moratorium Campaign.

Unfortunately they advertised it and 600–700 people attended. We did not know it at the time but the Federal Police had got the vice squad to dress up, grow beards and all that stuff and they came through the front gate, sixteen of them, and busted the function. The whole purpose behind this event was to raise funds to reimburse a young woman who had been courageous enough to put up her life savings to bail out four draft resisters charged with failing to fill out their draft papers for conscription into the army for two years. They absconded their bail conditions but were eventually arrested and processed through the courts. Breach of bail meant that the young woman lost her life savings. Why I am telling you that is because I was represented by a barrister that Mick O'Brien lined up who's name was Peter Faris.[4] I was charged with serving alcohol on a Sunday without a licence. I was also told by the Mayor of Fitzroy that if I was found guilty I would lose my job as the professional youth worker for Fitzroy. So I was under the pump.

Peter Faris got me off and I shouted him lunch and told him about the legal service I wanted to start in Fitzroy and he said, you've got me. It was he and one of his friends who had tried to start a shop front legal service in Smith Street, Remy Van de Wiel another barrister.[5] So we had two barristers.

I will never forget the public meeting. There was a lot of opposition to the starting of the Fitzroy Legal Service; there was a lot of opposition to creating a free legal service. So people from the legal profession came along to stop it getting off the ground. The public meeting split into two. There were fifteen young people under the age of eighteen who came along to talk about their stories of dealing with the legal system and the police. At that stage the police in Fitzroy, Carlton and Collingwood did not have a good reputation and they did not treat young people reasonably at all. The young people were there to try and get some legal representation and it looked like it was not going to work. Most of the leaders of the welfare organisations said there was enough welfare in the area and that they didn't want

---

4. Peter Faris (later QC) soon afterwards took the Fitzroy model to commence the Central Australian Aboriginal legal service. In 1989 he became chairman of the National Crime Authority, and in later years a famously confrontationist media commentator.

5. In 1972 Van de Wiel began a free legal service in the rear of the anarchists' 'Free Store' (Chesterman, 54–5)

another one and that a free legal service was just another one. The treasurer of the Law Institute said we didn't need it because we had the Legal Aid Committee and the young people jumped up and said they tried that and weren't eligible for it.

So the meeting split in two, those for and those against the legal service. We went into two separate rooms and those who wanted it said we were going to start it the next Tuesday. I believe that our public meeting was on Tuesday 5 December, after the election of the Whitlam Government on Saturday 2 December.

We started the Fitzroy Legal Service in the basement of the Fitzroy Town Hall, the temporary location of the Fitzroy Community Youth Centre which I was employed by at that time. Right beside it was the cells of the Fitzroy Police Station. So through the thick wall you'd hear thump and you knew what was going on so you'd kick and yell, and that would stop. So that was an interesting twist of fate.

I believe it was on the 18 December 1972 that the Fitzroy Legal Service opened its doors to provide legal service to the community. We had two barristers—Remy Van der Weil and Peter Faris—and myself. I did not want them to have a collar and tie because in my view you meet the disadvantaged more on their terms in regard to appearance so that they don't feel in awe of you. Also that in any legal interview we have, we have a non-lawyer present because clients won't understand the language used by lawyers, although they will nod that they understand because they are getting it for free, but in real terms they won't understand. So if the non-lawyer does not understand then the client won't understand. So the non-lawyer's role was to demystify the language between the lawyer and the client and not to have suits and not to sit on the other side of the desk but chair-to-chair. So they were to meet them as a person who had resources and knowledge that the consumer could utilise.

It was a bit of a radical concept but these two barristers said that they would do it so we had these two fellows rock up and we had two clients. The next day they were contacted by the media but the lawyers refused to talk to them because the bar counsel rules were that if you acted as a solicitor you'd be struck off for touting as a barrister. They could not afford to speak to the media about what they were doing. So it was left to me to face the media and two of the local television station (ABC TV Channel 2 and Channel 9) interviewed me and we were in the news. That same night, 20 December, we got twenty-five clients. We were working voluntarily underneath the town hall, in the same little office I used as the youth worker. There was a youth centre being built across the road but that took a couple of years. So we did not know what to do—because there were only myself, two other non-lawyer volunteers, and the two barristers. The next night there were fifty people, but the beauty was that it was stimulating a lot of socially conscious young lawyers who wanted to volunteer. The service was totally dependent on voluntary participation. Anyway it grew and it grew fast and within six weeks we were averaging 100 people a night, six nights a week, from 5.30pm to 11.00pm. The people would queue up in a line around the town hall and down the road. The queue was extraordinary. The unmet legal need was substantial.

The reason I had started the Fitzroy Legal Service was fundamentally for young people but we had cracked a nerve that there was a significant legal need right across the board. Issues then became substantive and within time I was spending a fair bit of time in other places where we set up other free legal services: Broadmeadows, Springvale, Nunawading, down in Geelong and North Melbourne. They were the ones I was involved with, and then I became Director of the Frankston Community Centre and started the Frankston Legal Service, which has become the Peninsula Legal Service. That was different in that I started with single women on the Pines Forest Estate.[6] Eighty-five per cent of those who lived on Pines Forest were single mothers, and there were lots and lots of children. We had a government at the time who designed an estate that was a ghetto. You had freeways all around it or private golf courses and stacks of kids. Of course the crime rates jumped through the roof and even led to attacks on the police station by the late 1970s—it was really tragic. The interesting thing is that this little legal service started by single-parent women inspired lots of people and is now really huge, and covers that whole region.

That's a basic history of the Fitzroy Legal Service. I will say that all the way through that period I had a fairly strong hand in the participation of other non-lawyers. About fifty per cent of the people

---

6. This Housing Commissions estate in Frankston North was situated in an area originally known as Pines Forest; the large estate soon became known as 'The Pines'.

involved were non-lawyers from the local area and beyond. Stacks of people with lots of skills, so we didn't just provide legal advice.

Ten years before Legal Aid started our practice was for barristers or lawyers representing clients to have their paying cases and the legal service cases on in the same courts. Which worked well, and also indicated the fantastic commitment of many lawyers who gave lots and lots of time, even though we might say many of those lawyers were appeasing their social conscience, because many of them were making lots and lots of money, and many of the people they were representing were as 'poor as'.

The other side of it was that it did generate law reforms in the area of consumer laws mainly, and pyramid selling. One example was Walton's. Walton's had their own currency and we challenged their money.[7] They would give people a $100 loan and in return would charge them interest on that loan and you can come and buy anything in our stores, they were department stores. It locked people in. You could pay it off at a weekly rate, say Au$5 a week which was fine but then at the end of each month there was interest put on what was outstanding and they would be charging interest on interest. They were tying poor people to their stores and their major focus was people from Housing Commission estates; they were operating substantially down the east coast of Australia.

What the legal service movement did was try to introduce financial counsellors and that started to become the beginning of the end of Walton's stores and lots of demonstrations started to occur. The beauty about it was that it was the women, mainly from the inner suburbs of Melbourne, and areas such as Broadmeadows, Heidelberg, Frankston and other public housing estates in the metropolitan areas of Melbourne who were the victims and were being exploited. Community legal centres began to spring up to meet this substantive legal issue impacting on the financial affairs of the disadvantaged. A Waltons Survival Kit was produced and distributed to consumers of Waltons stores. Demonstrations outside Waltons suburban stores developed. Legal challenges were made about the legality of Waltons stores money. Their monthly accounts were also challenged. For the first time financial counselling services were established inside the framework of community legal centres. The Trade Practices Act was

---

7. The YCW also ran a major campaign against Walton's.

also amended during this period and by the early eighties all these actions broke the back of Walton's itself.

It was a fantastic result and from that time on you probably know as much about Community Legal Services as I do—it is massive and right across Australia. But the Fitzroy Legal Service was the first and it had to fight fights that none of the others did because it had to fight the legal profession and also the welfare industry which were both opposed to setting up a free legal service.

I remember Lionel Murphy who was the Attorney General coming down. He was so impressed, and I wanted him to create a funding source across Australia for it, but he wanted to create the 'Australian Legal Aid Office'. He patted me on the shoulder and said, I know you probably don't agree with this John but I need some politics out of this for a lifeboat. So instead of giving the money to the people, which is very much Cardijn as far as I am concerned, he set up his government's structure. There is now no Australian legal aid office, but there are state legal aid structures. The words 'legal aid' are repulsive to me, always have been. It should be called 'Community Legal Services' and their focus should be empowerment.

Finally I wanted to say that in the 1980s I was involved with an organisation that I helped create, the Victorian Youth Advocacy Network. While working with young people in local areas, its focus was their human rights. This organisation flourished. By 1990 there were forty-one youth human rights organisations in local areas across Victoria. We had funding of $1.5 to $2 million and the interesting thing about this organisation was they had nine salaried workers and I was their co-ordinator but I was employed by young people under the age of eighteen. The young people were the ones who had the power and it was fantastic. Some of the stuff they did was brilliant. It was like what you could say it had a bit of a YCW flavour about it in its methodology and in the fact that it was run by young people not for them. The same stuff that Cardijn talked about.

Book Review
Of Labour and Liberty, Distributism
in Victoria 1891–1966

Stefan Gigacz

Catholics and Labor Party supporters may be surprised to learn that former ALP parliamentarian Race Mathews' latest book, *Of Labour and Liberty, Distributism in Victoria 1891–1966,* was originally written as a doctorate in theology thesis for Catholic Theological College, Melbourne, and the University of Divinity.

Although the title barely hints at it, the book traces the history of the influence of Catholic social thinkers and activists in the development of the Australian cooperative movement, particularly the cooperatives pioneered by the YCW (Young Christian Workers) movement in Melbourne.

In so doing, it builds on Mathews' earlier book, *Jobs of Our Own: Building a Stakeholder Society,* which sourced the origins of distributism—understood as widely distributed property ownership and particularly as exemplified in the successful Mondragon worker cooperatives—to the influence of Catholic social teaching and practice as it developed in Europe and Canada in the late 19th nineteenth and early twentieth centuries.

Why such interest in Catholic social teaching from a Fabian socialist and self-described agnostic? At one level, the answer no doubt lies in a citation quoted by Mathews' from the late ANU economist, Heinz Arndt, who wrote of a 1948 social justice statement drafted by the Australian National Secretariat for Catholic Action (ANSCA) that 'one could hardly find a more succinct statement of the point of view of intelligent, modern Democratic Socialists'.

Seventy years later, according to Mathews, such teaching has gained even greater relevance in the face of "a precipitous decline in active citizenship" consequent on 'a loss of confidence in politics and parliamentary democracy' combined with 'the inexorable creep and concentration of capital in the hands of the 'one per cent' minority'.

In this context, Mathews perceives distributism, and by extension Catholic social teaching and practice, as a 'possible antidote' to several 'convergent catastrophes' in the political, economic and environmental arenas 'that threaten to engulf' the world today.

Yet, whereas the Mondragon cooperatives founded by the Basque priest, Fr Jose Maria Arizmendiarrietta achieved 'triumphant success' in Spain, to Mathews' dismay and surprise, the Australian cooperative movement, which was greatly influenced by the pioneers of the YCW cooperatives, including Ted Long, Bob Maybury and Leon Magree, has largely disappeared.

Hence, Mathews' questions: First, what caused 'the failure of "First Wave" Australian Distributism to fulfil its promise'? Secondly, how to revive and build on a 'now all but forgotten political philosophy and program . . . as a means of bringing about a more equal, just and genuinely democratic social order'?

In seeking an answer to the first question, Mathews notes the seminal impact in the development of distributist philosophy of Pope Leo XIII's encyclical, Rerum Novarum, and the role of English Cardinal Henry Manning, both of whom greatly influenced Joseph Cardijn, the Belgian founder of the YCW.

In the Australian context, these ideas were taken up by Sydney Cardinal Patrick Moran, a great defender of worker rights who, according to Mathews, inspired the 1907 Harvester judgement enshrining the basic wage, and Archbishop Daniel Mannix in Melbourne.

A generation later, the Melbourne-based Campion Society also played a critical role in the promotion of Catholic social teaching under the leadership of Frank Maher, Kevin T Kelly, a key figure in the arrival of the YCW in Australia, and BA Santamaria.

In practical terms, however, it was the first generation leaders of the Melbourne YCW in the 1940s who put these teachings into effect. They did this by the establishment of a network of credit and consumer cooperatives that eventually became 'the largest and most lasting material attempt by the Melbourne Catholic Actionists to re-Christianise Australian society', as David Kehoe wrote in an unpublished history of the Melbourne YCW cited by Mathews.

The aim of all these efforts was 'to overcome the evils of unrestricted capitalism (which makes workers little better than slaves) and brutal socialism which destroys the dignity of the individual', as Melbourne Co-adjutor Archbishop Justin Simonds told a 1952 YCW cooperatives conference.

Mathews is clearly struck by the parallel role of the YCW in the development of cooperatives in Victoria with the role played in Spain by Arizmendiarrieta, who worked closely with the JOC leaders, in the development of the Mondragon cooperatives.

As Mathews notes, Mondragon is 'incontrovertibly a product of the Church's social teachings and YCW formation in the Cardijn mould'. But this raises the question as to why did the Victorian cooperative movement not continue to develop as its Spanish counterpart had done?

Here Mathews points to the conflicts of the 1940s and 1950s that opposed BA Santamaria's Catholic Social Studies Movement (CSSM) to the YCW. As he notes, Santamaria was not 'willing to concede any merit to the YCW's "See, Judge, Act" technique of changing essentially hostile environments through the transformation of individual consciences'. Instead, according to Mathews, the CSSM sought to implement 'top-down management and a militarised organisational model' that 'increasingly supplant(ed) (ANSCA's) former formation focus'.

Moreover, as he also pointedly notes, the YCW and the other specialised Catholic Action movements were chronically under-resourced. Thus, out of £5000 of funding allocated by the Australian bishops to Catholic Action in 1954, over £3550 went to the CSSM while the remaining £1450 was divided between the YCW, YCS and rural movement.

Other factors also later intervened which led to the decline of the Victorian cooperatives. Here, Mathews identifies the premature deaths of Archbishop Simonds and Fr Frank Lombard, founding chaplain of the Australian YCW. Secondly, later generations of YCW leaders became preoccupied with other issues. Finally, Mathews also hints at the lack of adult movements that could have carried forward the work initiated by the YCW leaders.

Moreover, Mathews in effect concludes that the Church failed to recognise the importance of the formation that the YCW had provided. And he transforms this critique into 'a way forward' in which 'under the new pontificate of Francis, awareness of the Church's moral critique of capitalism is re-kindled and Church rediscovers its rich heritage of concern for the rights and wellbeing of workers'.

'Seizing the day', Mathews proposes, the Australian bishops could move to promote 'a renewed and distinctively Distributist lay aposto-late such as that of the YCW cooperators in concert with the resurgent wider cooperative, mutualist and employee ownership movements and sympathetic elements within bodies including think tanks, trade unions and community groups'.

Drawing on the insights of Cardijn and Arizmendiarrietta, 'current and future priests' would receive more extensive coverage of Catholic social teaching and its 'significance in the context of the Mondragon experience' with 'absolute primacy' given to formation.

Jocist-style public enquiries might also be carried out with the objective of determining whether adaptations of Mondragon could be implemented in regional cities like Geelong, Wollongong or Rock-hampton.

This may be 'pure fantasy', Mathews concedes. 'Nevertheless, at a time when both the advocates of the statutory corporation school of State Socialism and their "greed is good" counterparts in the corporate sphere have simultaneously and comprehensively discredited themselves, the way is open for Distributism to assume the larger role to which its merits so plainly entitle it', he concludes.

Race Mathews makes an important contribution not only to labour and cooperative history but also to YCW and Church history in the 'Great South Land of the Holy Spirit', as he describes it echoing de Quiros.

Race Mathews, *Of Labour and Liberty, Distributism in Victoria 1891–1966* (Melbourne: Monash University Publishing, 2017).

Aus$34.95
<http://www.publishing.monash.edu/books/oll-9781925495331.html>

Remembering François Houtart

François Houtart

François Houtart 1925 - 2017

Many people would be surprised to learn that the introductory section on *The Human Condition in the World of Today* to the Vatican II Pastoral Constitution, Gaudium et spes, was originally drafted by an avowed Marxist.

Indeed, François Houtart, the Belgian priest and sociologist, who died this week at the age of 92, was close to many leaders of the Latin American left, ranging from Cuba's Fidel Castro, to Hugo Chavez of Venezuela, the Nicaraguan Sandinista leaders, Rafael Correa of Ecuador, and the Colombian guerilla priest Camillo Torres.

Perhaps he was simply following in the footsteps of his grandfather, the Belgian prime minister, Henri Carton de Wiart, who had been elected to parliament as a left-wing member of the Catholic Party in 1896.

Given this background, it may seem paradoxical to learn that Houtart was also friends for many years with the anti-communist Pope John Paul II. Their friendship began in 1947 when, as a young seminarian, Houtart hosted the equally young Polish priest, Fr Karol Wojtyla, on his first trip to Belgium.

Wojtyla had come to study the situation of the workers and learn about the work of a dynamic new movement founded by Joseph Cardijn known as the Jeunesse Ouvrière Chrétienne (JOC) or Young Christian Workers (YCW). On the same trip, he also visited France to learn about the emerging worker priests movement, many of whom also had close links to the JOC.

Houtart continued to accompany Wojtyla on the latter's later summer vacation trips to Belgium, visiting coal mines, factories and trade unions. They could not have then imagined that they would meet again in Rome between 1963 and 1965 to work together on the drafting of Schema 13, which was to be adopted by the Council as *Gaudium et Spes.*

In fact, both Houtart and Wojtyla took part in the Signs of the Times Sub-Commission, which was responsible for studying the situation of the world as the starting point for the document that would become *Gaudium et spes.* As the secretary of the Sub-Commission, Houtart played a key role in the compilation of material for the group.

It was in this capacity that he prepared the original draft introduction which can be read here:

http://testimonies.josephcardijn.com/1964---les-signes-des-temps

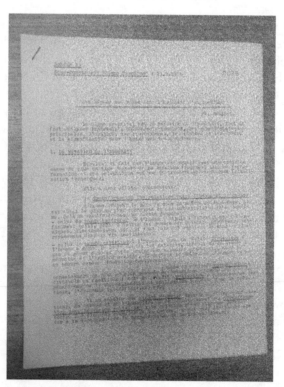

The original draft for the introduction to Gaudium et spes

As François later told me in an interview, the draft was based on a book that he had also published in 1964 entitled *L'Eglise et le monde* (The Church and the world).

Archbishop Wojtyla of Krakow, as he was by then, clearly appreciated Houtart's "beautiful book" and later explicitly praised Houtart's draft introduction as his letters illustrate.

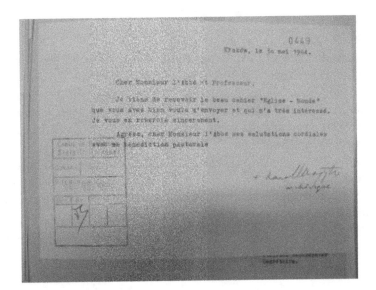

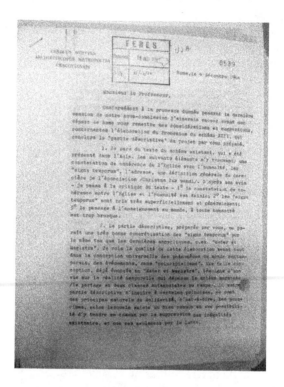

These were Wojtyla's comments on Houtart's draft:

Original

La partie déscriptive, préparée par vous, me paraît une très bonne con-
crétisation des "signa temporum" sur le même ton que les dernières
encycliques, p.ex. "Mater et Magistra". Je vois la qualité de cette élabo-
ration avant tout dans la conception universelle des phénomènes du
monde contemporain, des événements, sans "principialisme". Une telle
conception, déjà énoncée en "Mater et Magistra", témoigne d'une vue
sur la réalité temporelle qui dépasse le schéma marxiste /le partage en
deux classes antagonistes ou camps/. Si votre partie déscriptive s'inspire
à certains principes, ce sont des principes naturels de solidarité, c'est-
à-dire, les principes, selon lesquels existe un bien commun et une pos-
sibilité d'y tendre en commun par la suppression inégalités existantes, et
non pas seulement par la lutte.

Translation

The descriptive part prepared by you seems to me to be a very good concretisation of the "signa temporum" along the same lines as the latest encyclicals, e.g. Mater et magistra. I see the quality of your drafting most of all in the universal conception of contemporary world phenomena without "principialism." Such a conception, already foreshadowed in Mater et Magistra witnesses to a view of temporal reality that goes beyond the Marxist scheme /based on a split between antagonist classes or camps/. While your descriptive part is based on certain principles, they are the natural principles of solidarity, i.e. the principles according to which there exists a common good and a possibility of working in common towards this by the suppression of existing inequalities, and not just by struggle.

If nothing else, it illustrates that Wojtyla was certainly not a conservative on social and economic issues. Moreover, his comments on Houtart's text are particularly insightful although it is notable that he does not regard Houtart's draft as in any way Marxist.

Interesting also to note the future pope's praise for Houtart's emphasis on "the common good," an orientation the latter maintained right to the end of his life. Indeed, to the extent that the concept of common good is making a comeback in public debate, Houtart is probably a significant contributor.

As for Houtart's early draft, which provided the basis for discussion in the Signs of the Times Sub-Commission, despite many changes and additions, a number of key elements of the original structure survived into the final version of *Gaudium et Spes*.

Sadly that conciliar cooperation between he and Wojtyla did not last once the latter became pope. Indeed, the Church under Pope John Paul II came to oppose the work of many of those social action and theology of liberation pioneers, who had themselves been inspired by Houtart, not to mention Cardijn himself.

Houtart, Cardijn and the JOC

In fact, François Houtart had begun his work in Latin America in the early 1950s by preparing studies on the situation there for the JOC Internationale, sending reports to the International Secretariat in Brussels, making contacts for the movement, etc.

The network of priests and bishops developed through Houtart's work would later play a major at Vatican II particularly with respect to *Gaudium et spes*, and later in the emergence of the Latin American Bishops Conference (CELAM).

François described this influence of the JOC at the Council in the interview that I did with him in 2014.

https://youtu.be/grHUVYq7UZo

Here too is Houtart's own record of the origins of CELAM:

http://www.persee.fr/doc/assr_0335-5985_1986_num_62_1_2404

Although he highlights the roles of the jocist bishops, including Manuel Larrain of Chile and Helder Camara of Brazil, he makes no mention of his own vital role. Others, however, have not failed to do so, including André Corten here and Christian Smith here.

It would take volumes to record the work of François Houtart in Latin America not to mention other regions of the world, particularly Asia and Africa.

Cardijn himself early recognised his qualities. In fact, Cardijn wanted Houtart to succeed him as international chaplain of the JOC International, a post that was denied him by the refusal of the then archbishop of Malines-Brussels, the diocese to which he belonged. François told us this himself at a meeting of the JOCI international team to which we invited him to speak during the early 1990s.

During this period, he also cooperated with us in the development of an international enquiry as he had previously done in 1956 with an enquiry on the religious situation of young workers carried out in preparation for the first World Council in 1957.

From CETRI to the World Social Forum

Later while studying in Belgium, I ended up living at Louvain-la-Neuve in an apartment next to Houtart's own home, which was located in the Centre Tricontinental (CETRI) that he had created to promote research on world development issues, particularly with respect to the three continents of the Global South, namely South America, Africa and Asia.

François used to say mass regularly in the chapel of the Benedictine Sisters whose convent was also located nearby. He clearly had a strong devotion to the Eucharist that I found particularly impressive and moving given his open adhesion to Marxist thought.

He was always unfailingly generous with his time and availability. And I am sure that there are many students from around the world who could testify to the support he gave them.

At Louvain la Neuve, Helen, my wife, and I would drop by for a coffee or invite him over for dinner in an effort to get him to share more experiences from his truly extraordinary life. François' memoirs which he recently completed will surely offer insights into many key aspects of Church and world events during the 20th century.

To pick just one example of his many involvements, I remember dropping by at CETRI one Saturday afternoon to find a meeting in full progress. It turned out to be a committee organising an Alternative Davos meeting in 1999, which became the forerunner of the World Social Forum launched in Porto Alegre, Brazil in 2001.

I know that he was deeply moved in 2009 to receive the UNESCO Madangeet Singh prize for the promotion of tolerance and non-violence "for his exceptional efforts to promote social justice in the world."

The shock

Like many others, I was shocked and devastated when it was revealed in 2010 that he had admitted molesting a child cousin some 40 years before. This came at the very moment when he had just been nominated for the Nobel Peace Prize, which would certainly have crowned his life work.

Frankly, I think I would have struggled to believe the allegations had he not admitted them. Perhaps now that he is no longer with us the veil will be further lifted on this aspect of his life. Certainly he would not be the first historical figure whose achievements were marred by serious personal weaknesses.

In any event, there's no doubt that despite these failings, as serious as they were, François Houtart did an extraordinary amount of good, as the remarkable number of testimonies emerging in recent days clearly shows:

https://twitter.com/search?src=typd&q=fran%C3%A7ois%20houtart

https://www.google.fr/search?q=fran%C3%A7ois+houtart

Indeed, I wonder if there wasn't an element of repentance and reparation in the austere life and punishing schedule that he followed for so many years and decades.

How to conclude then?

Perhaps it's the former archbishop of Buenos Aires, yet another person with whom François Houtart once collaborated, who offers the best guide.

"All of us are sinners," Pope Francis reminds us. Instead of looking at the sins of others, "we should all look at our sin, our falls, our mistakes and look at the Lord."

Contributors

David Michael Kehoe BA (Hons) University of Melbourne, and researcher and author of History of the Melbourne YCW 1932–58.

Fr Bruce Duncan is a member of the Redemptorist Congregation and lectures at Yarra Theological Union in Box Hill in history and social ethics, particularly on Catholic social movements and ideas. His publications include *The Church's social teaching: from Rerum Novarum to 1931* (Melbourne: CollinsDove, 1991); *Crusade or Conspiracy: Catholics and the Anti-Communist Struggle in Australia* (Sydney: UNSW Press, 2001); and *Social Justice: Fuller Life in a Fairer World* (Melbourne: Garratt Publishing, 2012).

Stefan Gigacz worked for the YCW in Australia, the Asia-Pacific region and the International YCW. He coordinated a major history project for the International Cardijn Foundation from 1997-2000. During this period, he launched the Cardijn Project, an initiative to compile and publish online the writings of Joseph Cardijn, a project that continues today. A lawyer by training with two master's degrees, he is now completing a PhD thesis on Cardijn's role and impact on Vatican II.

As a young apprentice and YCW leader, John Finlayson met Cardinal Joseph Cardijn in 1966 and later he became a fulltime worker for the Melbourne YCW. As a youth worker, he became aware of the difficulties with the legal system faced by many young people. Together with other former YCW leaders and local lawyers, he founded the Fitzroy Legal Service, Australia's first community legal service. He later returned to the YCW as an adult collaborator. He also studied law and now works as a solicitor in Melbourne.

David Michael Kehoe graduated BA (Hons) in history from the University of Melbourne in 1976 and worked for nearly 30 years in the secular and religious media. The Melbourne YCW commissioned him in 1978 to research and write the history of the Melbourne YCW, 1932–1958.

Race Mathews is a former Chief of Staff to Gough Whitlam, Federal MP, Victorian MP and Minister, Local Government Councillor, academic, speech therapist and primary teacher. He has held numerous positions in the Australian Labor Party and the co-operative and credit union movements and has written and spoken widely about their history, attributes, and activities. A major focus of his research has been the great complex of worker-owned co-operatives at Mondragon in the Basque region of Spain and its origins in the social teachings of the Catholic Church. He is married to writer Iola Mathews, and lives in Melbourne.

Kevin Peoples was a member of the YCW in the Ballarat Diocese, Victoria, in the second half of the 1950s. He became the National Organising Secretary of the National Catholic Rural Movement in 1959. After studying for the priesthood in the 1960s at Springwood, New South Wales, he became a teacher with the Victorian Education Department. As a TAFE teacher in the ACT, he became the Federal President of the TAFE Division of the Australian Education Union of which he is a Life Member. He has a Master's Degree in Australian History from the University of Melbourne. Kevin is a member of the Victorian Greens and in his retirement has written two books and has another coming out in October, 2017. The theme of this book is Church Culture and Sexual Abuse in the Catholic Church.

Helen Praetz is Professor Emeritus at RMIT University where she was Pro Vice-Chancellor Teaching and Learning and chaired the government's Victorian Qualifications Authority. She has also worked as a teacher, policy analyst and public servant. She has published three books on Catholic education and articles on post compulsory schooling, qualifications and inequality.

Peter Price gained his Phd in History at Monash University in 2010 where his thesis considered English responses to the First Vatican

Council. He has been a senior lecturer in Church History at Yarra Theological Union and is an adjunct Senior Research Fellow with Monash University in Melbourne. Peter is married to Judy, with three adult family members and five grandchildren.

Rev Dr Max Vodola is a priest of the archdiocese of Melbourne and head of the Department of Church History at Catholic Theological College, East Melbourne (University of Divinity). Max lectures in the history of the Church in Australia and has maintained an interest for many years in Cardijn, YCW and Catholic Action.

Style Guide for submissions
Cardijn Studies journal:

Setup

Remove all additional 'returns' from document. Use only one return at the end of each paragraph. Only insert an additional return if there is a specific reason such as a break in stanzas of poetry.

Remove all 'tabs' in the document. If you need to offset a line, eg for quoting poetry, then do so by setting a tab in paragraph setup, not by repeatedly hitting the tab key or spacebar.

Use only one space at the end of a sentence.

Use the font Times New Roman, or Times, 12 point for body, double spaced. Use 10 point for footnotes.

Spelling and Punctuation

Use UK spelling conventions. The main differences in UK spelling apply to words with suffixes such as *–ise* and *–our*. Refer to Oxford Dictionary. Retain original spelling in quotations.

Use UK punctuation conventions. The main differences in UK punctuation apply to quoting, where single quotes are used, and the close quote is placed prior to the final punctuation (unless the quote comprises the totality of the sentence). Use of the 'Oxford comma' is encouraged.

Note the difference between a hyphen - , en-dash – , and em-dash — .

Use en-dash between page numbers, dates, and verses: 607–11; 1906–1945; vv. 12–15.

Use em-dash between phrases: He wondered—as he often did.

Only use a hyphen for hyphenated words eg: eco-ethic. UK spelling convention generally prefers the use of hyphens for readability.

Do not use the automatic ellipsis. Instead, use 3 periods with a space between each (...). If the ellipsis includes a period which concludes a sentence, there should be 4 periods.

Refer to Chicago Manual of Style for clarification of punctuation marks, and for correct abbreviations, numbering etc.

Referencing

Use numbered footnotes (with no bibliography) using a footnote function.

Use longform for the first appearance of a reference, and shortform for subsequent references eg Bethge, *Dietrich Bonhoeffer*, 73. Refer to the Chicago Manual of Style 16th Ed. for further details.

Final Preparation

During the peer review phase any corrections to layout, punctuation, spelling and referencing may be drawn to your attention for correction before acceptance by the publisher.

CPSIA information can be obtained
at www.ICGtesting.com
Printed in the USA
FSHW02n1236061018
52710FS